St. Ignatius' Own Story
As told to Luis González de Cámara

With a sampling of his letters

LOYOLA UNIVERSITY PRESS
is pleased to make
this out-of-print book
available once again
to its old friends

This book* is a

Loyola
request
reprint

St. Ignatius' Own Story

As told to Luis González de Cámara

With a sampling of his letters

Translated by William J. Young, S.J.

LOYOLA UNIVERSITY PRESS
Chicago 60657

Introduction

Here is St. Ignatius' own story, with the authentic tone and clear strength which characterize the direct statements of the Saints. Reading it, we see the man in his true quality and watch the molding of his firmly knit nature into the great lover of Christ and loyal knight in His service which divine grace produced by its strange, sure ways. Brief as it is, this account creates a memorable picture of Iñigo Loyola, the spirited Basque nobleman who left to himself would have been perhaps a soldier honorably remembered in a small sector of the Pyrenees, but who in fact gave up the opportunity. What he did accomplish shook his generation and went on to change the course of history by the powerful action of a current he set up, a force which mingled with many others but guided them too, an impact which is still shaping the human drama.

One would not suspect this importance from the story as Ignatius gives it. He tells only the events of his life, with no trumpeting of their significance. The story stops in mid-course, and there is little light from it on the historic founding of the Society of Jesus, which was to carry on Ignatius' work and spirit down the centuries. To those who are aware, however, of what Ignatius' *Spiritual Exercises*, his new kind of religious Order, his special approach to the Catholic apostolate have meant to the Church and to modern history, it is fascinating to see here the seeds of so much change and persisting activity. At least Pope Paul III realized the implications early. In approving Ignatius' work and plans, in 1540, he remarked "The finger of God is here." (Pastor, *History of the Popes*, 12.33.) It *was* a new creation, and it was primarily God's doing.

For long, Ignatius was quite unaware of the goal to which grace was leading him. He knew only that he loved God above all things, and that he could entrust himself entirely to God's guidance. He followed the tutelage with heroic loyalty and with a confidence in divine goodness and wisdom which is beyond the vision of selfish and self-satisfied men. Perhaps his example in this regard is Ignatius' chief value to our day. God knows how the world's problems and its terror of self-destruction would fade away if we all lived by Ignatius' norms!

This account of his life was extorted from the Saint by the affectionate importunity of his friends. Fathers Nadal and Luis González de Cámara, his close assistants and secretaries, put pressure on Ignatius for several years to recount his earlier life for the benefit of his Jesuit sons. The Saint found many excuses—ill health, "more important things to do," and a certain amount of Spanish delaying tactic: *mañana*. Finally de Cámara's insistence won a promise of compliance, and in September of 1553 Ignatius began. With various interruptions, his story was told to de Cámara up to October 20, 1555, when the secretary was sent off from Rome on business. Within a few months, Ignatius died (July 31, 1556).

The narrative is presented in the third person: "he" and "the Pilgrim" mean Ignatius throughout. Father de Cámara obtained Ignatius' story by oral narration. He promptly put this into writing, with great care for accuracy and with no admixture of his own comments, views, or explanations. Most of the manuscript is in Spanish, but the final part (¶ 79 on) is in a rather poor Italian. The style is essentially Ignatius' own, a simple and unpretentious account of events, with few revelations of his personal feelings. But the stature of his inner life could not be hid, and a careful reading of his experiences and conduct shows the depth of Ignatius' faith and how total was his conquest of himself. It shows a Saint in the making—a fascinating, if somewhat awesome, spectacle.

We can trace in the story a notable development of that profound and clear understanding of the psychology of the spiritual life which makes Ignatian spirituality distinctive. His own experience of temptations, scruples, and delusions built up his principles for the "discretion of spirits" and eventually made him a master guide to others on the difficult road to high perfection. It is easy to discern here the germinal ideas of the *Spiritual Exercises,* that remarkable little book which has had such lasting influence on Catholic thought and life these past four hundred years. It is evident, too, that Ignatius had mystical experiences so exalted and so frequent that he deserves to be recognized as one of the great mystics of the Church. The fact that he was Canonized in company with St. Teresa of Avila is a symbolic reminder of that fusion in him of practicality in action with sublimity of divine union for which she is more widely appreciated.

Ignatius' account breaks off toward the end of 1538. His greatest achievements in organizing the Society of Jesus and in drawing up its Constitutions and setting its distinctive spirit and traditions came after that date. His early companions did not need information on those familiar events, but Father de Cámara did get from the Founder some concluding secrets on the writing of the *Exercises* and the Constitutions. The active role played in this by divine guidance is impressively revealed in the final pages of Ignatius' story.

The Latin translation of de Cámara's autograph, made very early by Father Annibale Coudreto (Decoudray) and revised by Father Nadal (St. Ignatius' chief assistant), under the title *Acta Quaedam Reverendissimi Patris Ignatii de Loyola, Pri-*

marii Secundum Deum Institutoris Societatis Iesu, was first published by the Bollandists in 1731 in volume VII of the *Acta Sanctorum* for July. The original Spanish and Italian text was first printed in 1904, in the *Monumenta Historica Societatis Iesu,* and again in vol. 66 of the same series, 1943. Two English translations appeared in 1900, by E. M. Rix in London and by J. F. X. O'Conor, S.J., in New York. Both were made from the Latin translation.

The present version is the first in English from the original texts. It is the work of a veteran translator deeply versed in the life and thought of St. Ignatius. Most appropriately, it appears in the Ignatian Year, as a contribution to the worldwide celebration of the Saint's death four centuries ago on July 31, 1556.

A sampling of St. Ignatius' letters is also here given. His correspondence was immense, filling thousands of pages in the *Monumenta Ignatiana.* In these letters of advice, government, and spiritual counsel we see St. Ignatius in action. The picture gained from the "Autobiography" is thus notably filled out. Much light is thrown on the spiritual principles which formed Ignatius' inner life. His remarkable insight into religious realities is everywhere revealed, and his dexterity in guiding others away from confusion or danger and on to closer union with God. To appreciate his skill as an administrator, we need to examine his official correspondence with Jesuits pioneering in the Order's work in many lands. These letters are not given here; they deserve larger treatment by themselves. The selections in this book should serve to indicate, however, many other facets of the Saint's character and outlook. They are arranged chronologically, beginning with his days at the University of Paris. The famous Letter on Obedience is included, and every reader will readily see why it has become a classic exposition of that difficult virtue.

There is much known about St. Ignatius beyond the details in his own account. Many of the early Jesuits wrote about the Founder and his work, and there is abundant documentation for his later life and activity. This fuller picture may be found in the standard lives of St. Ignatius. There are many of these in English, culminating in the masterful biography by Father James Brodrick, S.J. (London, 1956). The reader of St. Ignatius' brief "autobiography" will want to go on to the larger lives also. But this short narrative by the Saint himself will always remain fundamental. It is a boon to have it available now in this clear and reliable translation.

Reading the lives of the Saints opened up for the wounded knight Ignatius a new vision of life, an appreciation of how noble a destiny and how exalting a challenge man has in the service of Christ our Lord. Reading St. Ignatius' own story could well have a similar inspiration for us. If we will only cooperate with grace, with something of his generosity, this little book will have won for the Captain Christ new volunteers to help spread His beneficent Kingdom in our time.

RAYMOND V. SCHODER, S.J.

Contents

LETTERS

The Life of Father Ignatius
as first written by Father Luis González
who received it from the lips of
the Father himself.

Author's Preface

1   One Friday morning of the year 1553, it being August 4th and the eve of Our Lady of the Snows, the Father was standing in the garden near the house or the room which is called the Duke's, when I began to give him an account of some of the particulars of my soul. Among other things, I spoke to him of vainglory. The Father suggested as remedy the frequent referring of all my affairs to God, making a serious effort to offer Him all the good there was in me, recognizing it as belonging to Him, and giving Him thanks for it. He spoke in a way that consoled me very much, so that I could not hold back my tears. The Father related to me how he had struggled against this vice for two years, to the extent that when he took ship in Barcelona bound for Jerusalem, he did not dare tell anybody that he was going to Jerusalem.[1] He acted the same way in other particulars, and, what is more, he added that he had enjoyed great peace of soul on this point ever afterwards. An hour or two after this we went to table, and while Master Polanco and I were eating, our Father told me that Master Nadal and others of the Society had often made a request of him, but that he had never made up his mind about it; but that after he had spoken with me, thinking the matter over in his room, he felt a great inclination and devotion to do so. He spoke in such a way as to

show that God had greatly enlightened him about his duty so to do, and that he had for once and all made up his mind. That request was to make known all that had taken place in his soul up to that moment. He had also decided that it was I to whom he was going to make these things known.

2 At the time, the Father was in very bad health, and was not accustomed to promise himself life from one day to the next. In fact, when he heard anyone saying, "I will do this two weeks from now, or a week from now," the Father was always a bit amazed: "How's that? Do you count on living that long?" And yet, on this occasion, he said that he hoped to live three or four months so as to bring this matter to an end. The other day I spoke to him and asked him when he wished to begin. He answered that I should remind him every day (I don't remember how many) until he was ready. But as business prevented him, he had me remind him of it every Sunday. It was then in September (I don't recall the day), that the Father called me and began the narrative of his whole life, recounting his youthful excesses clearly and distinctly with all their circumstances. Later in the same month he called me three or four times, and carried his story up to within a few days of his stay at Manresa, as will be seen in the part written by a different hand.

3 The Father's way of telling his story is what he uses in all things. It is done with such clearness that it makes the whole past present to the beholder. There was no need, therefore, of putting any questions, for the Father remembered and told whatever was worth knowing. I went at once to write it out, without a word to the Father, first in notes in my own hand, and later at greater length as it now stands. I have taken pains not to insert any word that I did not hear from our Father, and if there is anything in which I am afraid of having failed, it is that by not wishing to depart from the words of the Father, I have not been able to explain clearly the meaning of some of them. I kept writing in this way until

September of 1553, as I have said. But from then on, after the arrival of Father Nadal, October 18, 1554, the Father constantly kept excusing himself because of some illness or the various engagements which turned up, saying, "When this matter is finished, remind me"; and when that was finished, he kept saying, "Now we are busy with this. When it is finished, remind me."

4 When Father Nadal arrived, he was delighted to find that we had begun, and bade me importune the Father, often telling me that the Father could in nothing do more good to the Society than in this, that this was really to found the Society. He too, therefore, frequently spoke to the Father, and the Father told me that I should remind him when they finished the business of the endowment of the college. But when that was finished, he had to go on with the affair of Prester John,[2] and the mail was ready to leave. On the ninth of March we began to take up the history. But at once, Pope Julius became dangerously ill and died the 25th. Then the Father kept putting it off until we had a new pope who, as soon as he was named, also fell ill and died (Marcellus).[3] The Father delayed until the creation of Paul IV,[4] and then, what with the great heat and his numerous occupations, he kept holding off until the 21st of September, when arrangements began to be made for my transfer to Spain. For these reasons I urged the Father to make good his promise, and so he arranged for a meeting on the morning of the 22nd in the Red Tower. When I finished Mass I went to him to ask whether it was time.

He answered me to go and wait for him in the Red Tower,[5] so that I should be there when he came. I understood that I should have to wait for him there. But while I was delaying in a passageway, to answer the questions of one of the brethren about some matter of business, the Father came and reproved me because I had overstepped the limits of obedience and failed to be waiting for him. He would do nothing that

day. But we brought great pressure to bear upon him. . . .
As a result, he returned to the Red Tower and dictated as
he walked, as he always did. But I kept drawing a little closer
to him so that I could see his face, and the Father told me
to observe the rule. Growing negligent, I drew near him and
fell into the same fault two or three times. He told me about
it and went off. At length he returned, so that in that same
Tower he finished dictating what has been written. But as
I was on the point of beginning my journey, the preceding day being the last on which the Father spoke to me about
this matter, I did not have time to write out everything at
length at Rome. And because I did not have a Spanish secretary at Genoa, I dictated in Italian the points I had jotted
down and brought with me from Rome. This writing I finished at Genoa in December 1555.

Chapter 1

1   Up to his twenty-sixth year he was a man given over to the vanities of the world, and took a special delight in the exercise of arms, with a great and vain desire of winning glory. He was in a fortress [1] which the French were attacking, and although the others were of the opinion that they should surrender on terms of having their lives spared, as they clearly saw there was no possibility of a defense, he gave so many reasons to the governor that he persuaded him to carry on the defense against the judgment of the officers, who found some strength in his spirit and courage. On the day on which they expected the attack to take place, he made his confession to one of his companions in arms. After the assault had been going on for some time, a cannon ball struck him in the leg, crushing its bones, and because it passed between his legs it also seriously wounded the other.

2   With his fall, the others in the fortress surrendered to the French, who took possession, and treated the wounded man with great kindliness and courtesy. After twelve or fifteen days in Pamplona they bore him in a litter to his own country. Here he found himself in a very serious condition. The doctors and surgeons whom he had called from all parts were of the opinion that the leg should be operated on again and the bones reset, either because they had been poorly set

in the first place, or because the jogging of the journey had displaced them so that they would not heal. Again he went through this butchery, in which as in all the others that he had suffered he uttered no word, nor gave any sign of pain other than clenching his fists.

3   His condition grew worse. Besides being unable to eat he showed other symptoms which are usually a sign of approaching death. The feast of St. John drew near, and as the doctors had very little hope of his recovery, they advised him to make his confession. He received the last sacraments on the eve of the feast of Sts. Peter and Paul, and the doctors told him that if he showed no improvement by midnight, he could consider himself as good as dead. The patient had some devotion to St. Peter, and so our Lord wished that his improvement should begin that very midnight. So rapid was his recovery that within a few days he was thought to be out of danger of death.

4   When the bones knit, one below the knee remained astride another, which caused a shortening of the leg. The bones so raised caused a protuberance that was not pleasant to the sight. The sick man was not able to put up with this, because he had made up his mind to seek his fortune in the world. He thought the protuberance was going to be unsightly and asked the surgeons whether it could not be cut away. They told him that it could be cut away, but that the pain would be greater than all he had already suffered, because it was now healed and it would take some time to cut it off. He determined, nevertheless, to undergo this martyrdom to gratify his own inclinations. His elder brother was quite alarmed and declared that he would not have the courage to undergo such pain. But the wounded man put up with it with his usual patience.

5   After the superfluous flesh and the bone were cut away, means were employed for preventing the one leg from remaining shorter than the other. Many ointments were ap-

plied and devices employed for keeping the leg continually stretched which caused him many days of martyrdom. But it was our Lord Who restored his health. In everything else he was quite well, but he was not able to stand upon that leg, and so had to remain in bed. He had been much given to reading worldly books of fiction and knight errantry, and feeling well enough to read he asked for some of these books to help while away the time. In that house, however, they could find none of those he was accustomed to read, and so they gave him a Life of Christ and a book of the Lives of the Saints in Spanish.

6   By the frequent reading of these books he conceived some affection for what he found there narrated. Pausing in his reading, he gave himself up to thinking over what he had read. At other times he dwelt on the things of the world which formerly had occupied his thoughts. Of the many vain things that presented themselves to him, one took such possession of his heart that without realizing it he could spend two, three, or even four hours on end thinking of it, fancying what he would have to do in the service of a certain lady, of the means he would take to reach the country where she was living, of the verses, the promises he would make her, the deeds of gallantry he would do in her service. He was so enamored with all this that he did not see how impossible it would all be, because the lady was of no ordinary rank; neither countess, nor duchess, but of a nobility much higher than any of these.[2]

7   Nevertheless, our Lord came to his assistance, for He saw to it that these thoughts were succeeded by others which sprang from the things he was reading. In reading the Life of our Lord and the Lives of the Saints, he paused to think and reason with himself. "Suppose that I should do what St. Francis did, what St. Dominic did?" He thus let his thoughts run over many things that seemed good to him, always putting before himself things that were difficult and important

which seemed to him easy to accomplish when he proposed
them. But all his thought was to tell himself, "St. Dominic
did this, therefore, I must do it. St. Francis did this; therefore, I must do it." These thoughts also lasted a good while.
And then other things taking their place, the worldly thoughts
above mentioned came upon him and remained a long time
with him. This succession of diverse thoughts was of long
duration, and they were either of worldly achievements which
he desired to accomplish, or those of God which took hold
of his imagination to such an extent, that worn out with the
struggle, he turned them all aside and gave his attention to
other things.

8   There was, however, this difference. When he was
thinking of the things of the world he was filled with delight, but when afterwards he dismissed them from weariness,
he was dry and dissatisfied. And when he thought of going
barefoot to Jerusalem and of eating nothing but herbs and
performing the other rigors he saw that the saints had performed, he was consoled, not only when he entertained these
thoughts, but even after dismissing them he remained cheerful and satisfied. But he paid no attention to this, nor did he
stop to weigh the difference until one day his eyes were
opened a little and he began to wonder at the difference and
to reflect on it, learning from experience that one kind of
thoughts left him sad and the other cheerful. Thus, step by
step, he came to recognize the difference between the two
spirits that moved him, the one being from the evil spirit, the
other from God.

9   He acquired no little light from this reading and began to think more seriously of his past life and the great need
he had of doing penance for it. It was during this reading
that these desires of imitating the saints came to him, but with
no further thought of circumstances than of promising to do
with God's grace what they had done. What he desired most
of all to do, as soon as he was restored to health, was to go

to Jerusalem, as above stated, undertaking all the disciplines and abstinences which a generous soul on fire with the love of God is wont to desire.

10   The thoughts of the past were soon forgotten in the presence of these holy desires, which were confirmed by the following vision. One night, as he lay awake, he saw clearly the likeness of our Lady with the holy Child Jesus, at the sight of which he received most abundant consolation for a considerable interval of time. He felt so great a disgust with his past life, especially with its offenses of the flesh, that he thought all such images which had formerly occupied his mind were wiped out. And from that hour until August of 1553, when this is being written, he never again consented to the least suggestion of the flesh. This effect would seem to indicate that the vision was from God, although he never ventured to affirm it positively, or claim that it was anything more than he had said it was. But his brother and other members of the family easily recognized the change that had taken place in the interior of his soul from what they saw in his outward manner.

11   Without a care in the world he went on with his reading and his good resolutions. All the time he spent with the members of the household he devoted to the things of God, and in this way brought profit to their souls. He took great delight in the books he was reading, and the thought came to him to select some short but important passages from the Life of Christ and the Lives of the Saints. And so he began to write very carefully in a book, as he had already begun to move a little about the house. The words of Christ he wrote in red ink and those of our Lady in blue, on polished and lined paper in a good hand, for he was an excellent penman. Part of his time he spent in writing, part in prayer. It was his greatest consolation to gaze upon the heavens and the stars, which he often did, and for long stretches at a time, because when doing so he felt within himself a powerful urge

to be serving our Lord. He gave much time to thinking about his resolve, desiring to be entirely well so that he could begin his journey.

12   As he was going over in his mind what he should do on his return from Jerusalem, so as to live in perpetual penance, the thought occurred to him of joining the Carthusians of Seville. He could there conceal his identity so as to be held in less esteem, and live there on a strictly vegetable diet. But as the thought returned of a life of penance which he wanted to lead by going about the world, the desire of the Carthusian life grew cool, since he felt that there he would not be able to indulge the hatred he had conceived against himself. And yet, he instructed a servant of the house who was going to Burgos to bring back information about the Carthusian Rule,³ and the information brought to him seemed good. But for the reason given above, and because his attention was entirely occupied with the journey he was thinking of making at once, he gave up thinking about the Carthusians as it was a matter that could await his return. Indeed, feeling that he was pretty well restored, he thought it was time to be up and going and told his brother so. "You know, my lord, the Duke of Nájera is aware that I have recovered. It will be good for me to go to Navarette." The Duke was there at the time. His brother led him from one room to another, and with a great show of affection, begged him not to make a fool of himself. He wanted him to see what hopes the people placed in him and what influence he might have, along with other like suggestions, all with the intention of turning him from the good desire he had conceived. But, without departing from the truth, for he was very scrupulous about that, he reassured him in a way that allowed him to slip away from his brother.⁴

Chapter 2

13   Thus, as the pilgrim mounted his mule, another[1] of his brothers wished to accompany him as far as Oñate. Him he persuaded on the way to make a vigil in the chapel of our Lady of Aranzazu.[2] During the night he prayed here for fresh strength on his journey. He left his brother in Oñate in the home of a sister[3] whom he was going to visit, while he himself went on to Navarette. He thought it would be good to collect a few ducats which were owed him in the house of the Duke, and so wrote a note to the treasurer. The treasurer answered that he had no money on hand, but when the Duke heard of it, he said that he might lack for everything else, but not for Loyola. The Duke wished to place him in charge of one of his properties, should he wish to accept it, in recognition of the reputation he had earned in the past. He got his money and left word for it to be distributed to certain persons to whom he felt some obligation, and applied part of it to a statue of our Lady which was poorly attired and which he wanted to see very well set up and adorned. Then, taking leave of the two servants who had accompanied him, he mounted his mule and left Navarette for Montserrat.

14   An experience befell him on the way which it would be good to recount. It will help to an understanding of how our Lord dealt with this soul who, although still blind, had

a great desire to serve Him to the best of his knowledge, and was set on performing great penances, not so much with an idea of satisfying for his sins, as to placate and please God. Thus, when he remembered to do some penance which the saints had performed, he resolved to do the same and even more. All his consolation was in these thoughts. He never took a spiritual view of anything, nor even knew the meaning of humility, or charity, or patience, or discretion as a rule and measure of these virtues. His whole purpose was to perform these great, external works, for so had acted the saints for God's glory, without thought of any more particular circumstance.

15   Well then, as he went on his way, he came upon a Moor riding a mule. They both fell to talking, and the conversation turned on our Lady. The Moor admitted that the Virgin had conceived without man's aid, but could not believe that she remained a virgin after once having given birth, and for this opinion submitted the natural reasons which occurred to him. For all the arguments which the pilgrim gave against this opinion, he could not refute it. The Moor then took the lead with such haste that he was soon lost to view, and left the pilgrim with his own thoughts of what had taken place. These gave rise to emotions that brought on a feeling of discontent in his soul, as he thought that he had failed in his duty. This in turn led to indignation against the Moor, as he thought that he had done very ill to allow a Moor to say such things against our Lady, and that he was obliged to defend her honor. Hence a desire arose to go in search of the Moor and give him a taste of his dagger for what he had said. This battle of desires lasted for some time with the pilgrim quite doubtful at the end as to what he ought to do. The Moor, who had gone on ahead, had said that he was going to a place which was on the same highway, a little further on, but a little to the side of the highway. The royal highway, however, did not pass through the place.

16   Tired out from this examination as to what it would be good for him to do, and not being able to come to any clear decision, he thought of letting the mule decide, and gave her a free rein up to the spot where the road divided. If the mule took the road that led to the village he would search out the Moor and give him a taste of his dagger. If she did not take the village road, but continued on the royal highway, he would leave him in peace. This he did. But it was our Lord's will that, although the village was only thirty or forty steps away, and the road to it broad and even, the mule took the royal highway and passed by the village road.

Before reaching Montserrat he arrived at a large town where he bought the clothing he had made up his mind to wear when he went to Jerusalem. It was some sacking of a very loose weave and a rough prickly surface, and he at once gave orders for a long garment reaching to his feet to be made of it. He bought a pilgrim's staff and a small gourd and attached it all to the mule's saddle.

17   He continued his way to Montserrat, thinking as usual of the great deeds he was going to do for the love of God. As his mind was filled with the adventures of Amadis of Gaul and such books, thoughts corresponding to these adventures came to his mind. He determined, therefore, on a watch of arms throughout a whole night, without ever sitting or lying down, but standing a while and then kneeling, before the altar of our Lady of Montserrat, where he had made up his mind to leave his fine attire and to clothe himself with the armor of Christ. Leaving, then, this place, he continued, as was his wont, thinking about his resolutions, and when he arrived at Montserrat, after praying for a while and making an engagement with his confessor,[4] he made a general confession in writing which lasted three days. He arranged with the confessor to have the mule taken away, and his sword and dagger hung in the church at the altar of our Lady. This man was the first to whom he had made known

his purpose, because up to then he had not revealed it to any confessor.

18   On the eve, then, of our Lady's Annunciation, March 24th, at night, in the year 1522, he went as secretly as possible to a poor man, and removing his fine clothes gave them to him, put on his desired attire, and went to kneel before our Lady's altar. Alternating between kneeling and standing, with his pilgrim's staff in his hand, he thus spent the whole night. At daybreak he left, and to avoid being recognized, he took, not the highway that led straight to Barcelona where he would meet many who knew him and honored him, but byways by which he came to a small town called Manresa, where he decided to spend a few days in the hospital and to make a few notes in his book which he carried very carefully with him and which brought him many consolations.

By the time he had covered about three miles from Montserrat, he was overtaken by a man who came after him in great haste to ask whether he had given some clothing to a poor man, as the poor man said he had. Answering that he had given the clothes, tears of compassion started from his eyes, compassion for the poor man to whom he had given his clothing, compassion for him because he had been suspected of stealing them. But no matter how much he tried to avoid esteem, he could not be long in Manresa before the people were saying great things about him, a report having got abroad from what happened at Montserrat. It was not long before they were saying more than was true, that he had given up a large income, and such things.

Chapter 3

19   Every day he begged alms in Manresa. He ate no meat, drank no wine, although both were offered him. On Sundays he did not fast, and he drank the little wine that was given him. Because he had been quite delicate about caring for his hair, which in those days was quite the vogue—and he had a good head of hair—he made up his mind to neglect it and to let it grow wild, without combing or cutting it or covering it either day or night. For the same reason he allowed the nails of his hands and feet to grow, because here too he had been excessive. While he was in this hospital, it often happened to him in broad daylight to see something in the air close to him, which gave him great consolation because it was very beautiful. He could not make out clearly what the thing was, but somehow it appeared to have the form of a serpent. It was bright with objects that shone like eyes, although they were not eyes. He found great delight and consolation in looking at this thing, and the more he saw it the greater grew his consolation. When it disappeared it left him displeased.

20   Up to this time he had continued in the same interior state of great and undisturbed joy, without any knowledge of the inner things of the soul. Throughout the days when this vision lasted, or a little before it began, for it went on for

many days, there occurred to him a rather disturbing thought which troubled him by representing to him the difficulty of the life he was leading, as though he heard a voice within him saying: "How can you stand a life like this for the seventy years you have yet to live?" But this he answered also interiorly with great strength, feeling that it was the voice of the enemy: "You poor creature! Can you promise me even one hour of life?" In this way he overcame the temptation and remained at peace. This is the first temptation that came to him after what has been said above. It happened while he was entering the church in which he heard high Mass daily, as well as vespers and compline, which were always sung, and in which he found great spiritual comfort. As a rule he read the passion during the Mass, always preserving his serenity of soul.

21   But soon after the temptation just now related, he began to experience great changes in his soul. Sometimes his distaste was so great that he found no relish in any of the prayers he recited, or in hearing Mass, or in any kind of prayer he made. At other times everything was just the contrary, and so suddenly, that he seemed to have got rid of the sadness and desolation pretty much as one removes a cloak from the shoulders of another. Here he began to marvel at these changes which he had never before experienced, saying to himself: "What new kind of life is this that we are now beginning?" At this time he still spoke occasionally with a few spiritual persons who had some regard for him and liked to talk with him. For although he had no knowledge of spiritual things, he showed much fervor in his talk and a great desire to go forward in the service of God. There was in Manresa at that time a woman of many years, who for a long time had been a servant of God. She was known as such in many parts of Spain, so much so that the Catholic King had called her once to tell her something. This woman, meeting one day with this new soldier of Christ, said to him: "May

our Lord Jesus Christ appear to you some day!" He was surprised at this and, giving a literal meaning to her words, asked, "And how would Jesus Christ appear to me?" On Sundays he never missed his weekly confession and communion.[1]

22 But at this time he had much to suffer from scruples. Although the general confession he had made at Montserrat had been entirely written out and made carefully enough, there still remained some things which from time to time he thought he had not confessed. This caused him a good deal of worry, for even though he had confessed it, his mind was never at rest. He began, therefore, to look for some spiritual man who would cure him of his scruples, but without success. Finally a doctor of the Cathedral Church, a very spiritual man who preached there, told him one day in confession to write out all he could remember. He did so. But after confessing it his scruples returned, each time becoming more minute, so that he became quite upset, and although he knew that these scruples were doing him much harm and that it would be good to be rid of them, he could not shake them off. Sometimes he thought the cure would be for the confessor to tell him in the name of Jesus Christ never to mention anything of the past, and he wished that his confessor would so direct him, but he did not dare tell the confessor so.

23 But without his having said a word to him, his confessor told him not to confess anything of his past life unless it was something absolutely clear. As he thought that everything was quite clear, this direction was of no use to him and he remained always with his trouble. At this time he was in a small room which the Dominicans had given him in their monastery, where he continued with his seven hours of prayer on his knees, rising faithfully every midnight, and performing all the other exercises already mentioned. But none of them provided him with a cure for his scruples, although it was now some months that they had been afflict-

ing him. One day, when he was especially tormented, he began to pray and to call aloud to God, crying out in his fervor: "Help me, O Lord, since I find no help from men or from any creature. No trial would be too great for me to bear if I thought there was any hope of finding that help. Do you, Lord, show me where I can find it, and even though I should have to follow a little dog to find it, I would do so."

24   While these thoughts were tormenting him he was frequently seized with the temptation to throw himself into an excavation close to his room and adjacent to the place where he did his praying. But, knowing that it was a sin to do away with himself, he cried again: "Lord, I will do nothing to offend you," frequently repeating these words as he did the first. Here he recalled the story of a saint who to obtain from God something he much desired, went many days without eating until he got what he wanted. Giving a good deal of thought to this fact, he finally made up his mind to do the same thing, telling himself that he would neither eat nor drink until God did something for him, or he saw that death was approaching. For, if he saw himself reduced to the extremity of having to die if he did not eat, in that case he would ask for bread and food (as though in that extremity, he could either ask for it or even eat it).

25   He resorted to this one Sunday after having received communion, and went through the whole week without putting a morsel of food into his mouth. He omitted none of his ordinary exercises, even going to the divine office and praying on his knees from midnight on, and so forth. But on the following Sunday, which was his confession day, as he was accustomed to be very detailed with his confessor, he told him also that he had eaten nothing that week. The confessor bade him give up this abstinence, and although he was still strong, he obeyed his confessor, and that day and the next found himself delivered from his scruples. But on the third day, which was Tuesday, while he was praying,

he began to recall his sins, and so went on thinking of his
past sins, one after the other, as though one grew out of another, till he felt that it was his bounden duty to confess them
once again. As a sequel to these thoughts, he was seized with
a disgust of the life he was leading and a desire to be done
with it. It was our Lord's way of awakening him as it were
from sleep. As he now had some experience of the different
spirits from the lessons he had received from God, he began
to look about for the way in which that spirit had been able
to take possession of him. He therefore made up his mind,
which had become very clear on the matter, never to confess his past sins again, and from that day on he remained
free of those scruples, holding it a certainty that our Lord
in His mercy had liberated him.

26   Besides his seven hours of prayer, he busied himself
with certain souls who came looking for him to discuss their
spiritual interests. All the rest of the day he spent thinking
of divine things, those especially which he had either read
or meditated that day. But when he went to bed he received
great illuminations and spiritual consolations which made him
lose much of the time he had set aside for sleep, and that was
not much. He looked into this matter a number of times and
gave it some thought. Having set aside so much time for dealing with God, and besides that even all the rest of the day,
he began to doubt whether these illuminations came from the
good spirit. He concluded that he had better not have anything to do with them, and give the time determined on to
sleep. And this he did.

27   While he was carrying out his abstinence from meat,
without any thought of changing it, one morning as he got
up, a dish of meat appeared before him as though he actually saw it with his eyes. But he had no antecedent desire for
it. At the same time he felt within himself a great movement
of the will to eat it in the future. Although he remembered
his former resolve, he could not hesitate to make up his mind

that he ought to eat meat. Relating this to his confessor later, the confessor told him that he ought to find out whether this was a temptation. But he, examine it as he would, could never have any doubt about it.

At this time God treated him just as a schoolmaster treats a little boy when he teaches him. This perhaps was because of his rough and uncultivated understanding, or because he had no one to teach him, or because of the firm will God Himself had given him in His service. But he clearly saw, and always had seen that God dealt with him like this. Rather, he thought that any doubt about it would be an offense against His Divine Majesty. Something of this can be gathered from the five following points.

28   *First*. He had a great devotion to the Most Holy Trinity, and thus daily prayed to the Three Persons distinctly. While he was also praying to the Most Holy Trinity, the objection occurred to him as to how he could say four prayers to the Trinity.[2] But this thought gave him little or no trouble, as being something of only slight importance. One day while he was reciting the Hours of our Lady on the steps of the same monastery, his understanding began to be elevated as though he saw the Holy Trinity under the figure of three keys. This was accompanied with so many tears and so much sobbing that he could not control himself. That morning he accompanied a procession which left the monastery and was not able to restrain his tears until dinner time. Nor afterwards could he stop talking about the Most Holy Trinity. He made use of many different comparisons and experienced great joy and consolation. The result was that all through his life this great impression has remained with him, to feel great devotion when he prays to the Most Holy Trinity.

29   *Second*. Another time there was represented to his understanding with great spiritual delight the manner in which God had created the world. It had the appearance of some-

thing white out of which rays were coming, and it was out of this that God made light. But he did not know how to explain these things, nor did he remember well the spiritual illumination which at that time God impressed upon his soul.

Third. At Manresa also, where he remained almost a year, after he began to feel God's consolations and saw the fruit produced in the souls with whom he dealt, he gave up those outward extremes he formerly adopted, and trimmed his nails and hair. One day, in this town, when he was hearing Mass in the church of the monastery already mentioned, during the elevation he saw with the inner eyes of the soul something like white rays that came from above. Although he cannot explain this after so long a time, yet what he clearly saw with his understanding was how Jesus Christ our Lord is present in that most holy sacrament.

Fourth. When he was at prayer, he often and for a long time saw with the inner eyes the humanity of Christ. The shape which appeared to him was like a white body, not very large or very small, but he saw no distinction of members. He often saw this in Manresa. If he were to say twenty, or even forty times, he would not venture to say that it was an untruth. He saw it another time when he was in Jerusalem, and still another when he was on the road near Padua. He has also seen our Lady in like form, without distinction of parts. These things which he saw gave him at the time great strength, and were always a striking confirmation of his faith, so much so that he has often thought to himself that if there were no Scriptures to teach us these matters of faith, he was determined to die for them, merely because of what he had seen.

30   *Fifth.* Once out of devotion he was going to a church which was about a mile distant from Manresa, and which I think was called St. Paul. The road ran along close to the river. Moving along intent on his devotion, he sat down for a moment with his face towards the river which there ran

deep. As he sat, the eyes of his understanding began to open. He beheld no vision, but he saw and understood many things, spiritual as well as those concerning faith and learning. This took place with so great an illumination that these things appeared to be something altogether new. He cannot point out the particulars of what he then understood, although they were many, except that he received a great illumination in his understanding. This was so great that in the whole course of his past life right up to his sixty-second year, if he were to gather all the helps he had received from God, and everything he knew, and add them together, he does not think that they would equal all that he received at that one time.

31   After this had lasted for some time he went to kneel at a nearby cross to give thanks to God, where again appeared that vision which he had often seen and which he had never understood, that is, the object described above, which he thought very beautiful and which seemed to have many eyes. But he noticed that as it stood before the cross it did not have that beautiful color as heretofore, and he understood very clearly, with a strong assent of his will, that it was the evil one. Later it often appeared to him for a long time, but he drove it away with the pilgrim's staff he held in his hand and a gesture of contempt.

32   Once in Manresa he was ill with a high fever which brought him to death's door, and he felt sure that his soul was about to leave his body. At this moment the thought occurred to him that he was a just man. It annoyed him to such an extent that he did nothing but resist it and place his sins before his eyes. He had more trouble with this thought than with the fever itself, but he could not overcome it no matter how he tried to get the better of it. However, as the fever abated a little and he was no longer in immediate danger of death, he began to cry out to certain ladies who had come to visit him that for the love of God if ever they saw him at the point of death again, they should cry out and remind

him that he was a sinner and should remember the offenses he had committed against God.

33   On another occasion, when he was on his way from Valencia to Italy by sea, the rudder of the ship was broken by a mighty storm, and matters came to such a pass that in his own judgment and that of many other passengers they could not in the ordinary course of events escape death. He examined himself carefully and prepared for death, but could not have any fear because of his sins, or of being condemned. He had rather great confusion and sorrow for not having made a proper use of the gifts and graces that God our Lord had bestowed upon him.

Again in the year 1550 he was very ill, and he and many others thought that his last hour had come. This time, thinking about death, he found so much joy and so much spiritual consolation in the thought of dying that he melted into tears. This became so common with him that he often turned his thoughts away from death to avoid having so much of this consolation.

34   At the beginning of winter (1522), he came down with a very severe illness, and the town placed him in the house of the father of a certain Ferrera,[3] who was later in the service of Baltasar de Faria.[4] Here he was very attentively cared for, and many prominent ladies [5] of the town came to watch over him at night out of the devotion they felt for him. But even after his recovery from this illness, he remained quite weak with frequent stomach pains. For this reason, and also because the winter was very severe, they insisted that he dress properly, wear shoes and a hat, two dark gray jackets of a rough sort of cloth, with a headpiece that was half bonnet and half cap. At this time there were many days when he was very eager to hold forth on spiritual things, and to find those who were likewise interested in them. But the time was drawing near that he had set for his departure for Jerusalem.

35   Therefore, at the beginning of the year 1523 he left for Barcelona to take ship, and although several offered to accompany him, he preferred to travel by himself, since his whole purpose was to have God alone for refuge. One day he was beset by many who argued with him to take some companions on the grounds that he did not know Italian or Latin, and a companion would be of great help to him. He answered that even if the companion was the son or the brother of the Duke of Cardona [6] he would not travel in his company. He desired, he said, three virtues, faith, hope and charity. If he had a companion he would expect help from him when he was hungry, and he would thus trust in him, and be drawn to place his affection in him, when he wanted to place all this confidence and affection and hope in God alone. He spoke thus out of the fullness of his heart. In this state of mind he wished to embark, not merely alone, but without any provisions for the voyage. When they discussed the cost of passage, he obtained free passage from the shipmaster, since he was without money. But he was expected to bring aboard enough ship's biscuit to keep him, and would not be taken aboard on any other condition.

36   When it came time to arrange for this biscuit he suffered great scruples. "Was this the faith and the hope that you had in God, of His not failing you?" The thought caused him a great deal of annoyance, and at length, not knowing what to do, as there were probable reasons on both sides, he made up his mind to place himself in the hands of his confessor. Thus, he made known how great was his desire for perfection, and for the greater glory of God, and the reasons which caused him to doubt whether he should bring along anything for his support. The confessor decided that he should ask what was necessary and take it along with him. Asking it of a lady, she enquired where he was going. For a moment he doubted whether he should tell her, and finally did not dare tell her more than that he was going to Italy and Rome.

Taken by surprise, she said, "You want to go to Rome? Why, there's no telling how they return who go there," meaning to say that they who go to Rome get little spiritual profit from it. His reason for not saying that he was Jerusalem bound was his fear of vainglory, a fear that so afflicted him that he never dared to say what land he came from or to what family he belonged. Finally, he got on board with his biscuit. But when he came to the seashore, finding five or six *blancas*⁷ in his pockets, all that was left of what he had begged from door to door, as this was the way he used to get along, he left them on a bench there on the seashore.

37   He went aboard, having been in Barcelona a little more than twenty days. While he was still in Barcelona before embarking, he sought out as usual all spiritual persons, even those who were living at a distance in hermitages, to hold conversation with them. But neither in Barcelona, nor in Manresa, could he find anyone to help him as much as he wished. Except in Manresa, that woman mentioned above, who said that she asked God that Jesus Christ appear to him, was the only one who to him seemed to be deeply versed in the spiritual life. Therefore, after leaving Barcelona he lost for good this eagerness to seek out spiritual persons.

Chapter 4

38   So fresh a following wind blew that the trip from Barcelona to Gaëta was made in five days and nights; not, however, without great fear because of the rough weather. All through that land there was a dread of the pestilence, but the pilgrim, as soon as he disembarked, set out for Rome. Of those who sailed with him, a mother and her daughter, who was wearing boy's clothing, joined him, together with another young man. They went along with him because they too were begging their way. When they arrived at an inn, they found a great fire and many soldiers about it, who gave them something to eat and plied them with much wine, as though they wanted to warm them up. Then the travelers separated, the mother and daughter going upstairs to a room and the pilgrim and the young boy to the stable. But about the middle of the night he heard loud cries coming from upstairs, and getting up to see what was going on, he found the mother and the daughter below in the courtyard weeping and bewailing that an attempt had been made upon them. So angry did he become at this that he began to cry out, "Do we have to put up with this?" and similar expostulations, which he expressed with such effect that everybody in the house was amazed and no one offered to do him any harm.

The boy had already fled, but the three of them resumed their journey even though it was still night.

39   When they arrived at a town that was nearby, they found it closed, and not being able to enter it the three of them spent the night in a damp church. They were not permitted to enter the city in the morning, and they found no alms outside it, although they went to a castle which seemed nearby, where the pilgrim felt a weakness coming on him, as much from the sea voyage as from the rest of his experiences. As he was unable to proceed, he remained where he was, while the mother and her daughter went on to Rome. Many people left the city that day, among them the lady of the land.[1] When he heard that she was coming he presented himself to tell her that he was ill only from weakness, and asked her to be allowed to enter the city to seek some remedy. She readily granted his request. He began to beg throughout the city, gathered a good number of small coins, rested there for two days, resumed his journey and reached Rome on Palm Sunday.

40   Here whoever talked with him, knowing that he had come moneyless on his way to Jerusalem, tried to persuade him to give up the idea, suggesting many reasons why he would not find passage without money. But in his soul he had a great certainty, which would admit of no doubt, that he would find a way of getting to Jerusalem. He received the blessing of Adrian VI, and then left for Venice, eight or nine days after Easter. He took along with him six or seven ducats which had been given to him to defray his passage from Venice to Jerusalem. He had taken them because of the fear with which others inspired him of not being able to get to Jerusalem otherwise. But two days after leaving Rome he began to realize that accepting this money meant that he was losing the confidence he had had, and he worried much for having taken the ducats and thought it would be good to get rid of them. Finally, he made up his mind to

distribute them generously among those who presented themselves, who were usually poor. He did so in such a way that
when he reached Venice all he had left was a little change
which was necessary for that night.

41   During this journey to Venice he slept in the piazzas
because of the measures taken against the plague. Once it
happened that as he awoke in the morning, he met a man
who, seeing that he was alive, took to his heels with fright,
because he must have appeared extremely pale.

Continuing his journey he reached Chioggia, and from some
companions who had joined him he learned that they would
not be allowed to enter Venice. These companions decided
to go to Padua to get a health certificate and he went along
with them. But as they traveled at a good pace he could not
keep up with them, and they left him at nightfall in a large
field. While he was here Christ appeared to him as He was
accustomed to, as we have already described, and strength-
ened him considerably. With this consolation, the next morning, without forging a certificate as, I think, his companions
had done, he arrived at the gates of Padua and went in, the
guards making no demands of him. The same thing happened
when he left the city, at which his companions were taken
very much by surprise, as they had come to get a certificate
to go to Venice, about which he did not trouble himself.

42   On their arrival at Venice, the officials came to the
boat to examine all the passengers, one after the other. Him
alone they left undisturbed. In Venice he maintained himself
by begging, and slept in the Piazza of St. Mark. He did not
care to go to the house of the Ambassador of the Emperor,
nor to make any special effort to find something with which
to get along. He had a deep certainty in his soul that God
must give him the means of getting to Jerusalem, and this
gave him such confidence that no reasons or fears suggested
by others were enough to make him doubt.

One day a rich Spaniard met him and asked him what he

was doing and where he wanted to go. Learning his intention, he took him home for dinner, and kept him there for several days until arrangements were made for his departure. From his Manresa days the pilgrim had this custom that when he ate with anyone, he never spoke at table, unless to answer briefly; but he listened to the conversation and made note of some things, from which he later took occasion to speak of God. When the meal was over that is what he did.

43   That is why this good man with all his family took such a liking to him that they wanted him to remain with them, and made an effort to keep him in the house. His host himself brought him to talk with the Doge of Venice. When the Doge [2] heard the pilgrim, he gave orders to give him passage in the Governors' ship which was sailing to Cyprus.

Although many pilgrims had come to Jerusalem that year, many had returned to their own lands because of the recent fall of Rhodes. There were thirteen, however, in the pilgrim ship which left first, eight or nine waiting for the Governors' ship. While it was on the point of sailing, our pilgrim came down with a violent fever. It left him after giving him a few bad days. The ship was to leave the day he had taken a purgative, and the people of the house asked the doctor whether the pilgrim could embark for Jerusalem. He answered that he could, if he wanted to be buried there. He did embark, and left that day, and vomited so much that he felt very light, but began to make a complete recovery. Some on board ship were guilty of manifest indecencies which he very severely reproved.

44   The Spaniards who were along advised him against doing so, because the crew of the ship were thinking of abandoning him on some island. But it was our Lord's will for them to arrive quickly at Cyprus where, leaving that ship, they proceeded overland to another port which was called Salinas, about thirty miles distant, and there boarded the pilgrim ship, to which he carried no more for his upkeep than

the hope he had in God, just as he had done in the first ship. Throughout this time our Lord appeared to him very often, which gave him much strength and consolation; but he thought that he saw something that was large and round, as though it were of gold. This kept appearing to him from the time he left Cyprus until they reached Jaffa.[3] While they were making their way to Jerusalem, mounted on their little donkeys, as usual, a noble Spaniard by the name of Diego Manes, two miles before reaching Jerusalem, suggested with great devotion that since they would soon arrive at a spot from which they could see the Holy City, it would be good for all to prepare their consciences and make the rest of the way in silence.

45   The suggestion seeming good to all, each one began to recollect himself. Shortly before arriving at the spot from which they could see the city, they dismounted, because the friars, who had been expecting them, came with their cross. As he gazed upon the city, the pilgrim felt a deep consolation, which they all felt, according to their own testimony, together with a joyousness that did not appear natural. He felt the same devotion in his visits to the holy places.

It was his firm determination to remain in Jerusalem, perpetually visiting the holy places. But in addition to this devotion, he also proposed to be of help to souls. For this purpose he brought letters of recommendation to the Guardian, which he gave to him, telling him of his intention to remain there to satisfy his devotion. But he said nothing of his desire to benefit souls, for this he had told to no one, while he had often spoken freely of the first part of his plan. The Guardian told him that he did not see how he could remain, since the house was in such need that it could not support the friars, and it was for this reason that they had determined on sending some of the friars to the west with the pilgrims. The pilgrim answered that he wanted nothing from the house, but only someone to hear him when he came to confession.

At this the Guardian told him that they might be able to arrange things, but that he should wait until the provincial⁴ came, who was the chief superior of the Order and was at the time in Bethlehem.

46   The pilgrim remained satisfied with this promise, and set about writing letters to some spiritual persons in Barcelona. Having written one, he was at work on the second on the eve of the departure of the pilgrims when he was summoned to the provincial and the Guardian, the former of whom had returned. The provincial addressed him kindly and told him that he had learned of his good intention to remain in the holy places, and had given the matter careful thought. From the experience he had of others, he thought that it would not be wise. Many, he said, had entertained a like desire, some of whom had been taken prisoner, others died, and that his Order had been later obliged to ransom those who had been taken captive. For this reason, he should get ready to leave the next day with the other pilgrims. His answer was that he had made up his mind to stay, and was determined to let no reason prevent him from sticking to his resolve, giving him honestly to understand that although the provincial did not agree with him, if it was not a matter which obliged him under pain of sin, he would not give up his purpose out of any fear. To this the provincial replied that they had authority from the Apostolic See to dismiss or retain those whom they wished to dismiss or retain, and to excommunicate anyone who refused to obey. In his case they judged that he should not remain.

47   As the provincial was willing to show him the bulls which gave him power to excommunicate, the pilgrim said that there was no need of his seeing them, since he believed their reverences, and since they so judged with the authority conferred on them, he would obey. This done, he returned to where he had been before, and was seized with a great desire of again visiting Mount Olivet before leaving, since it

was not our Lord's will that he remain there in those holy places. On Mount Olivet there was a stone from which our Lord ascended into heaven and the print of His footstep is still to be seen. It was this he wished to see again. Without a word to anyone, therefore, or without taking a guide (for those who go without a Turk as guide run great risk), he slipped away from the others and went alone to Mount Olivet. The guards did not want to let him in, but he gave them a desk-knife which he carried with him. After having prayed with deep devotion, he wanted to go to Bethphage, and while he was there, he recalled again that he had not noticed on Mount Olivet in what direction the right foot was turned, or in what direction the left. Returning, he gave his scissors, I think, to the guards for permission to enter.

48   When they learned at the monastery that he had left without a guide, the friars made every effort to find him. As he was coming down from Mount Olivet, he fell in with a Syrian Christian who worked at the monastery. The man had a large staff and showing signs of great annoyance made as though he were going to beat him with it, and when he came up with him, grabbed him roughly by the arm, and the pilgrim easily allowed himself to be led away. The good man never let go of him. Coming thus in the grasp of the Syrian Christian, he had great consolation from our Lord Who he thought he saw above him all along the way. This consolation lasted in great abundance till they reached the monastery.

Chapter 5

49   They left on the next day,[1] and when they arrived at Cyprus, the pilgrims parted company and went on different ships. There were in the harbor three or four vessels bound for Venice. One of them was Turkish, another of them a very small vessel, and a third a very rich and heavy ship belonging to a wealthy Venetian.[2] Some of the pilgrims asked the master of this ship to take the pilgrim, but he, as he knew the pilgrim was without funds, would not do so, even though they renewed their instances and praised the pilgrim. The owner answered that if he were a saint he could travel as traveled St. James, or something of the kind. But the petitioners found it very easy to prevail upon the owner of the smaller vessel. They left one day in the morning with a favorable wind, but by afternoon they ran into a storm, which separated them, the great ship going down, close to the island of Cyprus, with only the passengers saved. The Turkish vessel and all on board were lost in the same storm. The small vessel had a hard time of it, but finally made Apulia, right in the midst of winter. It was very cold, and there was much snow. The pilgrim had no more clothes than some breeches made of coarse cloth which reached to the knee, leaving the rest of the leg bare, a jacket of black cloth, much slashed at the shoulders, and a short vest of light hair.

50   He arrived at Venice about the middle of January,
1524, having been at sea on his way from Cyprus all of the
months of November and December, and part of January. In
Venice he found one of the two men who had received him
into their homes before he sailed for Jerusalem, and was given
an alms of fifteen or sixteen julios and a large piece of cloth
which he folded several times over his stomach because of
the severe cold.

After the pilgrim understood that it was not God's will
that he remain in Jerusalem, he kept thinking on what he
ought to be doing, and finally felt more inclined to study
so as to be able to help souls. He then made up his mind to
go to Barcelona, and left Venice for Genoa. One day while
he was at his devotions in the principal church of Ferrara, a
poor man asked him for an alms, and he gave him a marquete,
which is equal to five or six quatrines. Later, another came,
and he gave him another small coin he had, but a little higher
in value. When the third came, he had nothing but julios,[3]
and he gave him one. As the poor saw that he was distribut-
ing alms, they did not stop coming until he had given away
all he had. Finally, a large number came together to ask an
alms, but he told them that they would have to pardon him,
as he had no more.

51   He then left Ferrara for Genoa. On the way he met
with some Spanish soldiery who that night treated him well.
They were very much surprised that he had come that way,
for he had to pass between both armies, the French forces
and those of the Empire.[4] They suggested that he avoid the
royal highway and take a safer one which they pointed out.
He did not, however, follow their advice, but continuing
straight on his way, came upon a town that had been burned
and destroyed, and until nightfall met with no one who gave
him anything to eat. But at sunset he came to a walled town
where the sentries took him into custody, thinking that he
was a spy. They put him in a hut close to the gate, and be-

gan to examine him, as they usually do with suspects. To all their questions he answered that he knew nothing. They stripped him and searched him even to his shoes, overlooking no part of his person, to see whether he was carrying any letters. But as they could in no wise learn anything from him, they were angry with him and led him to their captain. "He would make him speak." When he told them that they had taken away all his covering with his clothes, they would not return it to him, and led him away clad only in his breeches and jacket, as above described.

52   While they were on their way, the pilgrim remembered how Christ was led away, although there was no vision here as on other occasions. He was led through three main streets. He went without any sadness, rather with joy and satisfaction. He kept it as a practice to address anyone he met in the direct form of "you," finding devotion in the fact that Christ and the Apostles so spoke. As they went along the streets, he fancied that it would be good to give up that custom for the moment, and use the more elevated form of addressing the captain, with some lurking fear of the torture they might inflict on him. But he recognized this as a temptation, and told himself that he would not use the courtly manner of speech, nor show any reverence, nor even take off his cap.

53   Arriving at the captain's palace, they left the pilgrim in one of the lower rooms, and there the captain spoke to him for a while. But he answered without giving any sign of courtesy, in a few words, with a considerable pause between one and the next. The captain thought he was crazy, and said so to those who had brought him in: "This fellow has no brains. Give him his things and throw him out!" As he left the palace, he fell in with a Spaniard who was living there, who brought him home, and gave him something with which to break his fast and what was necessary for that night. He left in the morning, and walked until towards evening

two soldiers caught sight of him from a tower, and came down to examine him. They brought him to their captain, who was French and who asked him, among other things, where he came from. Learning that he was from Guipúzcoa, he said: "I am from nearby there,"—probably from the neighborhood of Bayonne—and then went on: "Take him along, give him something to eat, and treat him well."

On this journey from Ferrara to Genoa many other things of less importance befell him. He finally reached Genoa, where he was recognized by a Viscayan named Portundo, who on other occasions had spoken to him when he was in the service of the Catholic King. He helped to find him a ship bound for Barcelona, which ran great risk of being taken by Andrea Dória, who gave them chase, as he was then in the service of the French.[5]

Chapter 6

54   On his arrival at Barcelona he told Isabel Roser and Master Ardévol, who was then teaching grammar, of his inclination to study. Both thought very well of it, Ardévol offering to teach him without charge, and Isabel to supply him with what was necessary for his support. In Manresa the pilgrim had known a friar, a Bernardine, I think, a very spiritual man. With him he wished to remain to make greater progress in the spiritual life and even to be of help to souls. He, therefore, answered that he would accept their offer if he did not find what he wanted in Manresa. But when he went there, he discovered that the friar had died.[1] Returning to Barcelona he began his studies with great diligence. But there was one thing that stood very much in his way, and that is that when he began to learn by heart, as has to be done in the beginning of grammar, he received new light on spiritual things and new delights. So strong were these delights that he could memorize nothing, nor could he get rid of them however much he tried.

55   Thinking this over at various times, he said to himself: "Even when I go to prayer or attend Mass these lights do not come to me so vividly." Thus, step by step he came to recognize that it was a temptation. After making his meditation, he went to the Church of Santa Maria del Mar, near

the house of his teacher, having asked him to have the kindness to hear him for a moment in the church. Seated there,
the pilgrim gave his teacher a faithful account of what had
taken place in his soul, and how little progress he had made
until then for the reason already mentioned. And he made a
promise to his master, with the words: "I promise you never
to fail to attend your class these two years, as long as I can
find bread and water for my support here in Barcelona." He
made this promise with such effect that he never again suffered from those temptations. The stomach pains which he
had suffered in Manresa and were the cause of his taking to
shoes, left him, and he felt well enough in that regard from
the time he left Barcelona for Jerusalem. For this reason,
while he was still at his studies in Barcelona, the desire returned of resuming his past penances, and he began by making a hole in the sole of his shoes, which widened little by
little until by the time the cold of winter arrived, nothing
remained of the shoes but the uppers.

56   He finished the two years of study, during which
time they told him that he had made great progress. He was
then assured by his teacher that he could go on to the arts
course, and told by him to go to Alcalá.[2] But he had a doctor in theology examine him, who gave him the same advice.
Thus, he left alone for Alcalá, although I think he had already gathered some companions.[3] When he arrived at Alcalá, he began to beg and live on alms. One day, after he
had been living this way some ten or twelve days, a cleric
and some others who were in his company, seeing him thus
begging, began to laugh at him and to insult him, as they
usually do to those who being hale and hearty take to begging. At this moment the superintendent of the new hospital
of "Antezana," passed by, and feeling sorry for him, called
him and took him to the hospital, where he gave him a room
and all that he needed.

57   He studied at Alcalá about a year and a half. And because he arrived in Barcelona in Lent of the year 1524, where he studied two years, he arrived in Alcalá in 1526 and studied the logic of De Soto, the natural philosophy of Albert the Great and the Master of the Sentences (Peter Lombard). While he was at Alcalá, he worked at giving the Spiritual Exercises and in teaching Christian Doctrine, and by this means brought forth fruit to God's glory, for there were many persons who acquired a deep knowledge and taste for spiritual things. There were others who were variously tempted, like the man who wanted to scourge himself but could not, just as if someone were holding his hand.

There were other similar occurrences that caused much talk among the people, especially because of the crowds that came wherever he taught the catechism. As soon as he arrived in Alcalá, he made the acquaintance of Don Diego de Guia, who was living with his brother, and in the printing business and comfortably well off. They helped him with their alms to support the poor, and maintained three companions of the pilgrim in their house. Once when he came to ask alms, Don Diego told him that he had no money, but he opened a chest in which there were various things, bedspreads of various colors, some candelabra, and such things, all of which he wrapped in a sheet, and gave to the pilgrim, who lifted them to his shoulders and went off to bring succor to his poor.

58   As mentioned above, there was much talk through the country of the things that were happening in Alcalá, each one telling a different story. Reports reached the Inquisition at Toledo, some members of which came to Alcalá. The pilgrim was warned by their host that they were calling the companions the sack-wearers, or, I believe, the *illuminati*,[4] and that they were going to make hash of them. They began at once to make enquiry and investigate his manner of life, and finally returned to Toledo without sum-

moning him, although they had come for that sole purpose.
They left the trial to the Vicar Figueroa, who is now with
the Emperor. After a few days he called them, and told them
that an enquiry and investigation into their manner of life
had been made by the Inquisitors, and that no error had been
found either in their teaching or in their lives, and that therefore they could go on as they had been without any inter-
ference. But as they were not religious, it did not seem good
for them to be wearing the same habit. It would be good,
and they so directed, if two (pointing to the pilgrim and
Arteaga) dyed their clothing black,⁵ and the other two (Cal-
lixto and Cáceres) brown. Juanico, who was French, was allowed to remain as he was.

59   The pilgrim promised to follow his instructions. "But,
I do not know," he observed, "what use there is in these in-
vestigations. Just a few days ago a certain priest refused to
give communion to one of us, because he received every
week, and they have even made it difficult for me. We should
like to know whether we have been found in some heresy."
"No," answered Figueroa, "for if they had they would burn
you!" "They would burn you too," rejoined the pilgrim, "if
they found you in heresy." They dyed their clothing as they
were commanded, and for about fifteen or twenty days Figueroa commanded the pilgrim not to go barefoot but to wear
his shoes. This he did, as he found it easy to obey in matters
of this kind when he was given a command.

Four months later, the same Figueroa held another investigation concerning them. Besides the ordinary charges, I believe there was another occasion of a married woman of some
importance who had a special devotion for the pilgrim. To
prevent herself being recognized, she came veiled, as is the
custom in Alcalá de Henares, between two lights, to the hospital. On entering, she removed her veil and went to the pilgrim's room. But they did nothing this time, nor even after
the trial did they call him or say anything to him.

60 After another four months, when he was established in a small house outside the hospital, an officer of the law stood at his door and called him: "Come with me a moment." He brought him to the jail and told him not to leave until other arrangements were made. This was in summer, and as his movements in the jail were not much restricted, many people came to visit him, and he accomplished as much as he would have had he been free in the teaching of catechism and giving the Exercises. He never consented to call a lawyer or attorney, although many offers were made to him. He remembers especially Teresa de Cárdenas [6] who sent someone to visit him who made many offers of obtaining his release. But he accepted nothing, always answering with the words, "He for Whose love I came here will release me when it seems good to Him."

61 He was eighteen days in custody without any examination or knowing why. At the end of this time, Figueroa came to the prison, and questioned him on many points, including this, whether he had commanded the sabbath to be observed. He also asked him whether he was acquainted with two women, mother and daughter. He said that he was. And whether he had known of their departure before they actually left. This he denied under oath. The Vicar then laid his hand on the pilgrim's shoulder with every sign of joy and told him: "That is the reason for your being here." Among the many people who followed the pilgrim's talks, there was a mother and a daughter, both widows, the daughter very young and beautiful. They had made great progress in the spiritual life, especially the daughter. Although they were of noble birth, they had made a pilgrimage on foot to the veil of Veronica at Jaën, by themselves, but I don't know whether they begged their way. This started a great deal of talk in Alcalá, and Doctor Ciruelo,[7] who had some responsibility over them, thought it was the prisoner who had induced them to make the pilgrimage, and so had him arrested. As the prisoner

heard what the Vicar told him, he asked: "Would you like me to enlarge a little on this matter?" He answered, "Yes." "Well, then, you ought to know," said the prisoner, "that these two women had often insisted with me that they wanted to go through the whole world, serving the poor now in one hospital, now in another. I have always withdrawn them from such a resolve, since the daughter is so young and so beautiful, and so on, and I told them that when they wanted to visit the poor they could do so in Alcalá, and bear the Blessed Sacrament company." At the end of the conversation, Figueroa took his leave with his notary who had taken everything down in writing.

62   At this time Calixto was in Segovia, and learning of this imprisonment, he came at once, although but recently recovered from a serious illness, and bore him company in his prison. But the prisoner told him that it would be better to go and present himself to the Vicar. The Vicar received him kindly, and told him that he would send him to the prison since it was necessary for them to be there until the women returned, to see whether they confirmed the statements made. Calixto remained in the prison a few days only, as the pilgrim saw that he was doing himself more harm because of the poor state of his health, since he was not yet quite fully recovered. With the help of a doctor who was a good friend of his, he had Calixto released.

The pilgrim had remained forty-two days in confinement, at the end of which the devout ladies having returned, the notary came to the prison to read the sentence that set him free, but required him to dress as the other students and forbade him to speak on matters of faith for four years, that is, until they had studied more, since they had no knowledge of philosophy and theology. The truth is that the pilgrim was the most learned of them all, but what he knew was without a solid foundation. Whenever they examined him this was the first statement he usually made.

63 After this sentence, he did not clearly see what he should do; for apparently they had shut the door to his helping souls, and for no other reason than that he had not studied. Finally he made up his mind to go to Archbishop Fonseca and put his case in his hands.

He left Alcalá and found the Archbishop in Valladolid, gave him a faithful account of what had happened, and told him that although he was not in his jurisdiction, nor obliged to abide by the sentence, he would act according to the Archbishop's orders. In speaking with them he always used the direct second person, as he did with everyone. The Archbishop gave him a cordial reception, and when he understood that he wished to change to Salamanca, said that in Salamanca he also had a college [8] and friends, all of which he placed at his disposal, and gave orders that four gold crowns be given him as he left.

Chapter 7

64　When he arrived at Salamanca[1] he went to pray in a Church where a pious woman recognized him as belonging to the group, four of the members of which had already been there some days. She asked him his name and brought him to the inn where his companions were staying. When in Alcalá they passed sentence that they were to dress like students, the pilgrim answered: "When you bade us dye our clothing we did so; but we cannot now do what you bid us because we have not the means with which to buy them." The Vicar, therefore, himself provided them with clothes and headgear, and everything else like the rest of the students. Clad in this manner they left Alcalá.

In Salamanca he confessed at St. Stephen's to a friar of St. Dominic. One day, after he had been there some ten or twelve days, his confessor said to him: "The fathers of the house would like to talk with you." "In God's name," he answered. "Well, then," said the confessor, "it would be good for you to come and have dinner with us on Sunday. But I warn you of one thing: they will ask you many questions." On Sunday he came with Calixto, and after dinner, the subprior, in the absence of the prior, together with the confessor, and I think another friar, went with them to a chapel where the subprior began pleasantly enough to tell him what good reports he had heard of his life and practices—that he went about preaching like the apostles, and that he would be glad to know something more in detail of what he had heard. He began by asking him what studies he had made, and the pilgrim answered: "Of us all, it is I who have studied the most." He then gave him a clear account of the little he had studied and the poor foundation he had.

65   "Well, then, what is it you preach?" "We do not preach," replied the pilgrim, "but we speak familiarly of spiritual things with a few, as one does after dinner, with those who invite us." "But," asked the friar, "what are the things of God you speak about; that is what we should like to know." "We speak," answered the pilgrim, "sometimes of one virtue, sometimes of another, to praise it; sometimes of one vice, sometimes of another, to condemn it." "You are not educated," observed the friar, "and you speak of virtues and of vices? No one can speak of these things except in two ways, either because he has studied, or through the Holy Spirit. You have not studied; therefore, you speak through the Holy Spirit." The pilgrim kept cool at this, as this method of arguing did not meet with his approval. After a moment's silence, he said that there was no need of going further into the matter. But the friar was urgent. "Even now, when there are so many errors of Erasmus [2] about, and of others which have misled the world, you don't want to explain what you mean?"

66   "Father, I will not say more than what I have said, unless it be before my superiors who can oblige me to." Before this the friar had asked why Calixto had dressed as he did. He wore a short cloak, a broad hat on his head and carried a pilgrim's staff in his hand, and shoes that reached halfway up his leg. As he was very tall it made him appear deformed. The pilgrim related that they had been jailed in Alcalá, and had been commanded to dress as students. The hat he wore because of the excessive heat had been given to

him by a poor priest. Here the friar said as though through clenched teeth, "Charitas incipit a se ipsa" [sic]—Charity begins at home.

But coming back to our story, the subprior being able to get no further word from the pilgrim, said: "Well, remain here; we can easily see to it that you tell us all." The friars themselves departed with considerable haste. The pilgrim first asked whether they should remain there in the chapel, or whether they would prefer some other place. The superior told them to remain in the chapel. Straightway the friars saw to the locking of all the doors, and they opened negotiations, it seemed, with the judges. The two of them were meanwhile three days in the monastery without a word being said to them of justice. They took their meals with the friars in their refectory. Their room was nearly always full of friars who came to see them, and the pilgrims talked to them about the things they usually talked about. The result was that there was something of a difference of opinion among them, many showing themselves well disposed towards them.

67   At the end of three days a notary came and took them off to jail. They were not confined below with evil-doers, but in a higher room, which because it was old and unoccupied was very dirty. They put them both in chains, attached to the foot of each of them, the chain then being fastened to a post in the middle of the building. The chain was from ten to thirteen palms long, so that when one wished to move anywhere the other had to go along with him. All that night they lay awake. The next day when news of their imprisonment got abroad in the city, people sent to the prison what they both needed for proper sleeping and supplied all their needs abundantly. Many kept coming to see them, and the pilgrim continued his practice of speaking of God and so forth.

The Bachelor Frias came to examine them separately, and the pilgrim turned over to him all his papers, which were the Exercises, for examination. He asked them whether they had any companions, and he told him yes, and where they were, and they went after them at once, at the bidding of the Bachelor, and brought in Cáceres and Arteaga, but left Juanico, who later became a friar. But they did not place them above with the two, but below with the common criminals. Here too he preferred not to have a lawyer or attorney.

68 A few days later, they were summoned before four judges, the three doctors Sancrisidoro, Paravinhas and Frias, and the fourth the Bachelor Frias. By this time they had all seen the Exercises. They put many questions to him, not only about the Exercises, but on theology; for example, on the Trinity and the Blessed Sacrament, asking in what sense he understood these articles. First he made a short introduction, but being commanded by the judges to go on, he spoke in such a way that they had no fault to find. The Bachelor Frias, who in similar circumstances had always shown himself to be more severe than the others, proposed something that had to do with canon law. He was required to give an answer to all questions, and did so by always saying that he did not know what the doctors said about such things. Then they bade him explain the first commandment as he usually explained it. He began to do so and continued at such length and said so much about the first commandment that they had no desire to ask him more. Before this, however, when they were talking of the Exercises, they insisted much on one point alone which is at the beginning of the Exercises, and concerns when a thought may be a venial sin and when it may be mortal. Their difficulty was that he, being without training, should determine a point like that. He answered that they should determine whether the answer were correct or not. If it were not correct, condemn it. The end of it all was that they went off without having condemned anything.

69 Among the many who came to the prison to talk to him, there was a certain Don Francisco de Mendoza, who is

now Cardinal of Burgos. He came with the Bachelor Frias, and to his question as to how he felt in prison and whether he found the time heavy on his hands, he answered: "I will answer you as I answered a woman today who spoke words of compassion at seeing me a prisoner. I told her: 'In this you show that you do not desire to be a prisoner for the love of God. Why does prison seem so great an evil to you? I will tell you that there are not bars enough or chains enough in Salamanca but I would desire more for God's love.' "

It happened at this time that the prisoners of the jail all made their escape; but not the two companions who were there confined. When they were found there in the morning with the doors wide open, and the jail empty of prisoners, the fact gave great edification to all and caused a good deal of talk in the city. As a result, they were given for prison an entire palace which stood nearby.

70   After being in prison for twenty-two days they were called to hear their sentence. No error was found either in their life or in their teaching, and so they were allowed to continue as they had been doing, teaching catechism and speaking of the things of God, provided that they never defined what was mortal and what was venial sin, until they had studied four years longer. When the sentence was read, the judges gave signs of great affection, as though they wished to see it accepted. The pilgrim said that he would do all that the sentence required of him, but that he would not accept it, because without condemning him on any point, they closed his mouth to prevent his helping his neighbor in what he could. No matter how much the Doctor Frias, who showed great friendliness, urged the matter, the pilgrim said that as long as he was in the jurisdiction of Salamanca he would do as the sentence bade him.

They were at once released from custody. But after commending the matter to God, he began to think of what his course would be. He found great difficulty in remaining in Salamanca, because this prohibition against defining mortal and venial sin seemed to close the door to his helping souls.

71 And so he made up his mind to go to Paris to study.

When the pilgrim was debating in Barcelona as to whether he should study and how far, his whole object was whether after he had studied he should enter religion, or whether he should go on as he had been going through the world. When thoughts of entering religion came to him, the desire also came of entering an Order that had become relaxed and was in need of reform. He thought that he would thus have more to suffer, and at the same time God would perhaps come to their help, and give him likewise a deep confidence which would enable him to bear patiently the contumely and the insults that would be heaped upon him.

Well, all through the time of his incarceration at Salamanca, he was never without the same desires of helping souls, and to study to this end and to gather together a few who felt as he did and hold those he had gathered. Once he had made up his mind to go to Paris, he agreed with them that they should wait for him where they were, while he would go and see whether there was some way in which they could all carry on their studies.

72 Many important persons did what they could to keep him from going, but they could get nowhere with him. Before they were fifteen or twenty days out of prison, he left by himself, taking a few books along on a donkey.[3] When he arrived at Barcelona, all who knew him tried to dissuade him from passing over to France because of hostilities. They recounted many instances of atrocities, even going so far as to say that the French roasted Spaniards on spits. But he saw no reason for being afraid.

Chapter 8

73   So he left Spain, alone and on foot, and reached Paris some time in February. According to my reckoning, this would be in 1528 [1] or 1527. He put up at a house with a few Spaniards and went to Montagu [2] to study Humanities. He did this because they had made him pass on so swiftly in his studies that he found his foundations very shaky. He studied with young boys, going through the order and methods of Paris. On his arrival at Paris he was given twenty-five scudi by a merchant on a draft from Barcelona. This he gave for safekeeping to one of the Spaniards at that inn, who went through it in a short time, and had nothing with which to pay him back. Thus when Lent was over and the pilgrim had no money left, he himself having met his expenses and the other having spent it as already narrated, he was reduced to begging, and had to leave the house in which he had been living.

74   He was taken in at the hospital of St. James, [3] just beyond the church of the Innocents. This caused great inconvenience with his studies, because the hospital was a long distance from Montagu, and it was necessary to be home at the stroke of the *Ave Maria* to find the doors open, and not to leave in the morning before daylight. This made it difficult for him to be present at his lectures. There was another

handicap: he had to beg alms to support himself. It was now some five years since he had had any stomach pains, and he began to undertake greater penances and abstinences. Spending some time in this hospital and beggar's life, and seeing that he was making little advance in his studies, he began to think about what he ought to do. Noticing that there were some who served other regents in the colleges, and still had time for study, he decided to look for an employer.

75 He thought the matter over by himself and came to this conclusion, which was not without its consolation: "I will imagine that the teacher is Christ, and I will give to one of his students the name of St. Peter and to another the name of St. John, and so on through all the Apostles. If the teacher tells me to do something, I will fancy that it is Christ who tells me, and when one of the others commands me, I will think that it is St. Peter." He went to great pains to find an employer. On the one hand, he spoke to the Bachelor Castro, and on the other, to a monk of the Carthusians, who had wide acquaintance among the teachers and others. But they never found it possible to get an employer for him.

76 Finally, as he found no solution to his difficulty, a Spanish friar told him one day that it would be better to go each year to Flanders and lose two months, or even less, to bring back enough to enable him to study for the whole year. This suggestion he thought good, after commending it to God. Following this advice, he brought back enough each year from Flanders to get along on for the year. Once he went over to England and brought back a larger sum in alms than he had been accustomed to do in former years.

77 On his first return from Flanders, he began to give himself more intensely than usual to spiritual conversation, and at almost the same time he gave the Exercises to three, namely, Peralta, the Bachelor Castro, who was at the Sorbonne, and to a Basque at St. Barbara, named Amador. Great

changes were effected in these men, and they at once gave
all they had to the poor, even their books; they began to beg
alms through Paris and took up lodgings at the Hospital of
St. James, where the pilgrim had stayed earlier and which he
left for reasons already given. This caused something of an
uproar in the University, for the first two were persons of
some standing and very well known. Soon the Spaniards began to take up arms against the two teachers, but not being
able to get the better of them with reason and pleading to
return to the University, marched on them one day in crowds
with weapons in their hands and dragged them away from
the hospital.

78   They brought them to the University, and came to
an agreement on this point, namely, that after they had finished their courses they might carry out their purposes. The
Bachelor Castro later went to Spain, preached in Burgos for
a time, and became a Carthusian in Valencia. Peralta left for
Jerusalem on foot as a pilgrim. In these circumstances he was
taken in hand in Italy by a captain, a relative, who had means
of bringing him to the Pope and had a command laid on him
to return to Spain. These events did not take place immediately, but a few years later.

In Paris loud complaints were raised against the pilgrim, especially by the Spaniards, and our Master de Gouvea [4] claimed
that he had turned Amador's head. Amador was a student in
his college. He made up his mind, so he said, that the first
time the pilgrim appeared at Sainte-Barbe he would give him
a drubbing as a seducer of the students.

79   The Spaniard whom he had as one of his first companions, who had squandered his money without recompens-
ing him, left for Spain by way of Rouen. While awaiting
passage at Rouen, he fell sick. From a letter, the pilgrim heard
of his falling sick, and conceived the desire of going to visit
and help him, thinking also that in this union of souls, he

might induce him to leave the world and give himself entirely to the service of God.

In order to obtain this he wanted to make the twenty-eight leagues between Paris and Rouen barefoot and fasting from food and drink. While he was recommending this adventure in prayer, he was seized with a great fear, until he went to the church of St. Dominic and there determined to go as was said, when all the fear of tempting God passed away.

But on the next day, the morning of his departure, as he was getting up early, he was seized with so great a fear that he could hardly get his clothes on. In this conflict of emotion he left the house and indeed the city before daybreak. It continued with him as far as Argenteuil, which is a walled town a few miles from Paris on the way to Rouen, where the vesture of our Lord is said to be preserved. He passed by this town in the grip of that spiritual struggle, and as he began to climb a hill the dread began to slip from him and in its place came so great a joy and spiritual consolation, that he began to cry out through the fields and to talk with God. That night he spent with a poor beggar in a hospital, after having covered fourteen leagues. The next night he spent in a straw hut, and the third day he reached Rouen. All this time he had taken nothing in the way of food or drink and had walked barefoot, as he had planned. At Rouen he comforted the sick man, helped him board a ship bound for Spain, and gave him letters of introduction to his companions at Salamanca, viz., Calixto, Cáceres and Arteaga.

80   Not to have to refer again to these companions, they turned out as follows: While he was at Paris, he frequently wrote to them as he had agreed, but it was to tell them of the slight hope he had of their coming to Paris to study. He wrote, however, to Doña Leonora de Mascarenhas,[5] asking her to help Calixto with a letter to the Portuguese Court to obtain one of the scholarships which the King of Portugal

had established at Paris. Doña Leonora gave the letter to Calixto, and provided him with a mule and some money for the journey. He set out for the Portuguese Court, but never reached Paris. Rather, he returned to Spain, and then went on to India with some spiritual woman. Later he was back in Spain, and went a second time to India. He came back to Spain a rich man, which at Salamanca caused no little surprise to those who had known him earlier.

Cáceres returned to Segovia, which was his native city, and there began a life which seemed to indicate that he had quite forgotten his earlier resolutions.

Arteaga became a dignitary, and then after the Society was established at Rome, he was offered a bishopric in India. He wrote to the pilgrim asking that it be given to one of the Society. As this was declined, he went to Portuguese India, was consecrated bishop, and met with a very strange death. Having fallen ill, he happened to have two glasses of water for his refreshment in his room. One of the glasses contained water which the doctor had ordered, the other a corrosive sublimate, very poisonous, which being given him by mistake ended his life.

81   The pilgrim returned from Rouen to Paris, and found that he was the subject of much talk, because of Castro and Peralta, and that the Inquisitor had made enquiries about him. He went to the Inquisitor without waiting to be summoned, and told him that he had heard that he was enquiring about him. "I am ready for whatever you wish," he said. The name of the Inquisitor was Master Ory, a Dominican friar, and the pilgrim urged him to get through with his enquiry as soon as possible, as he wished to begin his course in Arts on the feast of St. Remy, and if this business were finished first he would be better able to get on with his studies. But all the Inquisitor had to say was that people had told him some things about him. He did not ask to see him again.

82   A short time after this, on the feast of St. Remy, October 1st, he began the course in philosophy under John Peña. He began it with the purpose of keeping with him those who had resolved on serving our Lord, but would not try to add to their number, as he wanted to give himself with greater ease to his studies.

Just as he began the lectures of his course, so also began once more the same temptations that beset him when he studied grammar in Barcelona. Whenever he attended lectures he could not, for the multitude of spiritual ideas that came upon him, fix his attention upon the lecture. Seeing that he was thus making little headway in his studies, he went to his teacher and gave his word that he would not fail to attend the whole course, if only he could find enough bread and water to keep himself alive. After making this promise, all these devotions which were so untimely ceased and he went on with his studies in peace. At this time he was associating with Master Peter Faber and Master Francis Xavier, whom he had won over to God's service through the Exercises. This interval of his course was free from the persecutions of other times. On this point Doctor Fragus once told him that he was surprised at the peace in which he lived, there being no one to annoy him. His answer was: "It is because I do not speak to anyone of the things of God, but once the course is finished the old life will return."

83   In the meantime, while they were talking, a friar approached Doctor Fragus to ask him to be good enough to help him find a house, because in that in which he lodged there had been many deaths which it was thought had been caused by the plague, because at that time the plague had begun to spread in Paris. Doctor Fragus and the pilgrim wanted to visit that house under the guidance of a woman who was very skilled in diagnosing the disease. She went into the house and said that it was plague-stricken. The pilgrim also entered, found a sick man there, comforted him, laying

his hand on the man's sore. After a few words of comfort and encouragement, he left by himself. His hand began to pain, and he thought that he had caught the plague. So strong did this fancy become that he could not control it, and he ended by thrusting his hand into his mouth, moving his fingers about, and telling himself: "If you have the plague in your hand, you'll also have it in your mouth." This done his imagination quieted down and the pain in his hand left him.

84   But when he returned to the College of Sainte-Barbe where he had lodgings and where he attended lectures, the inmates would not allow him to enter when they learned that he had gone into the plague-ridden house, and fled from him. He was thus obliged to spend several days outside.

They have a custom at Paris for those who are studying philosophy in the third year for a baccalaureate. It involves the expenditure of a gold crown, and consequently many poor students are not able to meet the expense. The pilgrim began to doubt whether it would be proper for him to take it. As he could come to no conclusion about his doubt, he decided to put the matter into the hands of his teacher. He advised him to take it, and so he did. Even so there were not lacking critics, in particular a Spaniard who made some remark about it.

During this part of his stay in Paris he suffered a great deal from his stomach. Every two weeks he had stomach pains which lasted a good hour and brought on a fever. Once the pains lasted some sixteen or seventeen hours. By this time, however, he had finished the course in philosophy, and had studied theology for several years and gathered about him a number of companions.[6] From then on the ailment continued to increase, and all the remedies they tried proved unavailing.

85   The doctors finally said that there was no other help for him than his native air. His companions gave him the same advice, and very earnestly urged him to follow it. By

this time they had come to some decision as to what they were going to do. Their plan was to go to Venice and from there to Jerusalem, where they were to spend the rest of their lives for the good of souls. If they were refused permission to remain in Jerusalem they would return to Rome, offer themselves to the Vicar of Christ, asking him to make use of them wherever he thought it would be more to God's glory and the good of souls. They proposed to wait a year in Venice before sailing, and if during that year there was no chance of taking passage for the East, they would be released from their vow to go to Jerusalem and could go to the Pope.

Finally, the pilgrim yielded to the persuasion of his companions. Those of them who were Spaniards had matters to settle at home which he would be able to manage. They agreed, therefore, that when he had fully recovered, he would go to negotiate their business, and then make his way to Venice, there to await his companions.

86   This was the year 1535, and according to their agreement the companions were to leave Paris in 1537, the feast of the Conversion of St. Paul (January 25th). But because of the war, they were forced to anticipate that date, and left in November of 1536. But just as he was about to leave, the pilgrim heard that an accusation had been lodged against him with the Inquisitor, and a process begun. Knowing this, and seeing that he had not been summoned, he went in person to the Inquisitor and told him what he had learned, that he was about to leave for Spain, and that he had associates. For this reason he asked him to pass sentence. The Inquisitor said that it was true there had been an accusation, but that he did not see that there was anything of importance in it. He only wanted to see what he had written in the Exercises. When he saw them, he praised them highly, and asked the pilgrim to leave him a copy. This he did. Nevertheless, the pilgrim

insisted that his case be brought to trial and that sentence be passed. But, as the Inquisitor seemed unwilling to do this, the pilgrim brought a public notary and witnesses to the Inquisitor's house and received formal testimony of the whole affair.

Chapter 9

87   This done, he mounted a small horse which his companions had provided, and started off alone for his native land, finding himself greatly improved along the way. Arriving at his own province, Guipúzcoa, he forsook the highway and took a more lonely mountain road. He had covered only a short distance when he came upon two armed men advancing towards him (the road had an ill name for cut-throats) who, after having passed him, returned and followed swiftly after. He felt a moment's fear. But accosting them, he learned that they were servants of his brother who had sent them out to look for him. It would seem that news about his arrival had come from Bayonne in France, where he was known. The two men set out, therefore, and he took the same road, coming upon them a bit before he entered his own country. They did all they could, but without success, to induce him to come to the home of his brother.[1] He went, therefore, to the hospital,[2] and then at a convenient hour sought alms throughout the town.

88   In this hospital he began to talk on divine things with many who came there to visit him, and by God's grace gathered no little fruit.[3] As soon as he arrived, he made up his mind to teach the catechism daily to the children. But his brother made strenuous objection to this, declaring that no-

body would come. The pilgrim answered that one would be enough. But after he began, many came faithfully to hear him, even his brother.

Besides the catechism, he also preached on Sundays and feast days with much fruit, some coming many miles to hear him. He also made an effort to remove some abuses, and with God's help he put order into some. For example, regarding gambling, he saw to it that regulations were made and enforced by those who were responsible for the administration of justice. There was also another abuse. In that country young girls went bareheaded and never wore anything on their heads until after they were married. But there were many who became concubines of priests and other men, and remained faithful to them as though they were their wives. This became so common that these mistresses had not the least shame in saying that they had covered their heads for so and so, and they were commonly known and acknowledged as such.

89   This custom gave rise to many evils. The pilgrim persuaded the governor to make a law that all those who had covered their heads for anyone but their lawful husbands, should be publicly punished. Thus a beginning was made in the removal of this abuse. He saw to it that some provision was officially and regularly made for the poor, and that the bells were rung thrice in the day, at the time of the angelus, morning, noon and evening, and that the people should pray as they do in Rome. At first he enjoyed good health, but soon fell seriously ill. He decided that when he recovered from this illness it was time for him to be on his way to accomplish the tasks laid upon him by his companions, and to set out without a penny. His brother took this very ill, as he was ashamed to see him thus traveling on foot and at evening. The pilgrim was willing to yield to him on this point, and ride a horse to the confines of the province accompanied by his brother and his relatives.

90   But when they reached the limits of the province, he got off the horse, and refusing all gifts, turned towards Pamplona, and from there went to Almazanum, the home of Laynez. From here he went to Sigüenza and Toledo, and from Toledo to Valencia. In all these homes of his companions he refused all gifts, although they were offered in great abundance and with great insistence.

In Valencia he spoke with Castro, who had become a Carthusian monk. He wanted to take ship for Genoa, but his well-wishers in Valencia begged him not to do so, because they said that Barbarossa [4] was at sea with a large fleet of galleys. Although they told him enough to frighten him, nothing they said caused him any hesitation.

91   He boarded a large ship, and survived the storm spoken of earlier (¶33) when he related the three times he was about to breathe his last.

On his arrival at Genoa, he took the road to Bologna, along which he had much to suffer, especially once when he lost his way and began to walk along a river bank. The river was deep and the road high, getting narrower the higher it went. Finally, it got so narrow that he could neither go forward nor turn back. So, he began to crawl on hands and knees and went on thus for some time with great fear, because every time he moved he thought that he would fall into the river. This indeed was the greatest of all physical efforts he had ever made. But he reached the end at last. Just as he was about to enter Bologna he slipped from a little wooden bridge and found himself as he rose covered with mud and filth. The bystanders, of whom there were many, had a good laugh at him.

From his entrance into Bologna he began to ask alms, but did not get even a single *quatrino*, although he covered the whole city. He stayed in Bologna some of the time ill, but afterwards went on to Venice using always the same method of travel.

Chapter 10

92   During those days in Venice he spent some time giving the Exercises and in other spiritual associations. The more important people to whom he gave them were Masters Peter Contarini [1] and Gaspar De Doctis, and a Spaniard called Rojas. There was also another Spaniard who was called the Bachelor Hocez, who had a good deal to do with the pilgrim and also with the bishop of Ceuta.[2] Although he had some desire to make the Exercises he never carried it into execution. Finally, however, he made up his mind to make them, and after the third or fourth day, opened his mind to the pilgrim to tell him that he had been afraid that some wicked doctrine was taught in the Exercises. Someone in fact had told him as much. It was for this reason that he had brought with him certain books which he could use as protection, if he happened to want to impose these doctrines on him. He found great help in the Exercises, and when they were over he resolved to follow the pilgrim's way of life. He was also the first to die.

93   In Venice also another persecution was begun against the pilgrim. There were many who said that his likeness had been burned in Spain and in Paris. Matters came to such a pass that a trial was held and sentence rendered in favor of the pilgrim.

The nine companions arrived at Venice in the beginning of 1537. There they separated to serve the sick in the different hospitals. After two or three months they all went to Rome to get the Pope's blessing before setting out on their journey to Jerusalem. The pilgrim did not go with them, because of Doctor Ortiz and the Theatine Cardinal who had just been created. The companions returned from Rome with drafts for two or three hundred *scudi* which they were given as alms to help them on their way to Jerusalem. They did not wish to receive the money, except in checks, and since they did not go to Jerusalem later, they returned the checks to those who had given them.

The companions returned to Venice just as they had left it, that is, on foot and begging, but divided into three parties, which were always made up of different nationalities. Those who were not priests were ordained in Venice, and received faculties from the Nuncio, who was in Venice at the time, and who was later called Cardinal Verallo. They were ordained under the title of poverty, all taking the vows of poverty and chastity.

94 During that year they could not find a ship for the Near East, because Venice had broken with the Turks. When they saw their hopes diminishing, they dispersed throughout the Domain of Venice, with the intention of waiting out the year they had decided upon, and then if there was no chance of getting passage, they would return to Rome.

It fell to the pilgrim to go with Faber and Laynez to Vicenza. There they found a house outside the city limits, which had neither door nor window, where they slept on a little straw they brought with them. Two of the three went twice daily to ask alms, and brought back so little that they could hardly subsist. Usually they ate a little toasted bread when they had it, prepared by the one whose lot it was to remain at home. In this manner they spent forty days intent on nothing but their prayers.

95   After the forty days, Master John Codure arrived, and the four of them decided to preach. They went to four different piazzas on the same day and at the same hour, and began to preach, first by shouting out to the people and waving their hats at them. This style of preaching started a great deal of talk in the city; many were moved to devotion and supplied their physical needs with greater abundance.

While he was in Vicenza he had many supernatural visions and much ordinary consolation, just the opposite of what he experienced in Paris. These consolations were specially given while he was preparing for ordination in Venice and getting ready to say his first Mass. In all his journeys he had great supernatural visitations of the kind he used to have when he was at Manresa. While he was in Vicenza, he learned that one of his companions who was staying at Bassano was sick and at death's door. He himself at the time was ill with a fever. Nevertheless, he started off and walked so fast that Faber, his companion, could not keep up with him. In that journey he was given the certainty by God, and so told Faber, that the companion would not die of that illness. When the pilgrim arrived at Bassano, the sick man was much consoled and soon got well.

All then returned to Vicenza, where all ten remained some days. Some went to seek alms in the towns adjacent to Vicenza.

96   As the year went by and they found no passage to Jerusalem, they decided to go to Rome, even the pilgrim, because the two persons about whom he doubted [3] showed themselves very kindly disposed on the other occasion when his companions had gone there.

They went to Rome in three or four groups, the pilgrim with Faber and Laynez, and in this journey he received many special favors from God.

He had made up his mind after taking orders to wait a year before saying Mass, preparing himself and praying our

Lady to place him with her Son. One day, a few miles before they reached Rome, while he was praying in a church, he felt such a change in his soul, and saw so clearly that God the Father placed him with Christ His Son, that he would not dare to doubt that the Father had placed him with His Son.[4]

(I who am writing these things told the pilgrim when he narrated this, that Laynez had recounted this occurrence with some added details. He told me that whatever Laynez said was true, because he did not recall all the particulars in such detail. But he added: "When I told him that, I knew for certain that all I told him was true." He made the same statement to me about other things.) [5]

97   Arriving at Rome, he observed to his companions that he noticed that all the windows were closed, meaning by that that they would have to suffer many contradictions. He also said: "We must walk very carefully and hold no conversations with women, unless they are well known." What happened to Master Francis is very pertinent here. At Rome he heard a woman's confession and visited her occasionally to talk about her spiritual life. She was later found to be pregnant. But it pleased God that the responsible party was caught. The same thing happened to John Codure whose spiritual daughter was caught with a man.

Chapter 11

98   From Rome the pilgrim went to Monte Cassino [1] to give the Exercises to Doctor Ortiz, and was there for forty days, during which he one day saw the Bachelor Hocez [2] entering heaven. He had many tears and deep spiritual consolation at this, and he saw this so clearly that if he said that he did not he would feel that he was lying. From Monte Cassino he brought Francis de Strada back to Rome with him.

Back at Rome, he worked helping souls, and still living at the vineyard [3] he gave the Spiritual Exercises to different people at one and the same time, one of whom lived near St. Mary Major, and the other near the Ponte Sesto. [4]

Persecutions now began, and Michael [5] started to be annoying and to speak ill of the pilgrim, who had him summoned to the governor's court, first showing the governor a letter of Michael's which praised the pilgrim highly. The governor [6] examined Michael, and put an end to the proceedings by banishing him from Rome.

Mudarra [7] and Barreda [8] opened their campaign of persecution. They alleged that the pilgrim and his companions were fugitives from Spain, Paris and Venice. In the end, both confessed in the presence of the governor and the legate who at the time was in Rome, that they had nothing wrong to say against them, either in their conduct or their teaching. The legate [9] imposed silence in the case, but the pilgrim was not satisfied with that, declaring that he wanted a definitive sentence. This was pleasing neither to the legate nor the governor nor those who at first favored the pilgrim. But after a few months, the Pope finally returned to Rome, and the pilgrim went to Frascati to speak with him, and gave him a number of reasons. The Pope, being thus informed, commanded that sentence be pronounced, which was done in favor of the pilgrim and his associates.

With the help of the pilgrim and his companions some works of piety were founded in Rome, such as the house of catechumens, the house of Santa Maria, and the orphanage. Master Nadal will be able to tell you all the rest.

99   After this recital, about October 20th, I asked the pilgrim about the Exercises, the Constitutions, wishing to learn how he drew them up. He answered that the Exercises were not composed all at one time, but things that he had observed in his own soul and found useful and which he thought would be useful to others, he put into writing—the examination of conscience, for example, with the idea of lines of different length, and so on. The forms of the election in particular, he told me, came from that variety of movement of spirits and thoughts which he experienced at Loyola, while he was still convalescing from his shattered leg. He said that he would speak to me about the Constitutions that evening.

That same day he called me before supper. He seemed to be more recollected than usual. He made a kind of protestation, the sum of which was to show the intention and the simplicity with which he had narrated these matters. He said that he was certain that he did not tell me anything beyond the facts, and that he had frequently offended our Lord after he had begun to serve Him, but that he had never given consent to a mortal sin. His devotion always went on increasing, that is, the ease with which he found God, which was then greater than he had ever had in his life. Whenever he wished, at whatever hour, he could find God. He also said he still had many visions, especially that in which he saw Christ as a sun, as mentioned above. This often happened to him, especially when he was speaking of matters of importance, and came to confirm him in his decision.

100   He also had many visions when he said Mass, and very frequently when he was drawing up the Constitutions. This he could affirm the more easily because he had the habit of setting down his thought every day, and these writings he had then found. He showed me a rather large bundle of collected writings, a large part of which he read to me. The larger part of the visions he saw in confirmation of some of the Constitutions, seeing now the Father, now all Three Persons of the Trinity, sometimes our Lady who interceded for him and sometimes confirmed what he had written.

In particular he told me of a decision on which he spent forty days, saying Mass each day, and each day shedding many tears. What he wanted to decide was whether our churches should have an income, and whether the Society could accept help from it.

101   His method of procedure, when he was drawing up the Constitutions, was to say Mass every day, and to lay the point he was treating before God, and to pray over it. He always made his prayer and said his Mass with tears.

I wanted to see all the papers dealing with the Constitutions, and I asked him to let me see them for a moment. But he would not.[10]

Letters

To Isabel Roser

Isabel was a noble and well known matron of Barcelona. Her husband, Juan Roser, was a business man of some means, of holy life, and both he and his wife were busy with good works. One day Isabel, listening to a sermon in the church of Santa Maria del Mar, saw St. Ignatius seated on the altar steps among the children, his face all aglow. Struck by his grave and modest demeanor, she called him to her home and invited him to dinner. The saint accepted the invitation, and spoke to her and her husband of the things of God with such warmth, that from that moment they both remained very much attached to him and helped him considerably with their alms. Ignatius is answering three letters he received from Isabel. He first thanks her for an alms she has given him, and then comforts her on the death of another pious woman whose name was Canillas, and accepts the excuses of others who at the time were unable to help him. He then goes on to show that God frequently heals the soul by afflicting the body, and closes by exhorting Isabel to practice virtue even in the face of difficulties.

Paris, November 10, 1532

IHS

May the grace and love of Christ our Lord be with us.

I received from Dr. Benet your three letters and the twenty ducats with them. May God our Lord be pleased to give you

73

credit for this on the day of judgment, and repay you for me, as I am sure He in His divine Goodness will do in new and sound money. I hope that He will not have to punish me for ingratitude, if in some way He makes me worthy of giving some praise and service to His Divine Majesty.

You speak in your letter of God's will being fulfilled in the banishment and withdrawal of Canillas from this life. In truth, I cannot feel any pain for her, but only for ourselves who are still in this place of endless weariness, pains and calamities. I knew that in this lifetime she was dearly loved by her Creator and Lord, and I can easily believe that she will be well received and entertained. She will have little desire for the palaces, the pomps, the riches and the vanities of this world.

You also mention the excuses of our sisters in Christ our Lord. Indeed, they owe me nothing, and it is I who am eternally indebted to them. If they see fit to employ their means otherwise for the service of God our Lord we should rejoice. But if they are unwilling or unable, I should really desire to have something to give them so that they could do much for the service and glory of God our Lord. As long as I live I cannot but be their debtor, and I am thinking that after we have finished with this life, they will be well repaid by me.

In your second letter you tell me of your long drawn out pain in the illness you have undergone, and of the great stomach pains that still remain. Indeed, I cannot help feeling the liveliest sympathy with you in your sufferings, seeing that I desire every imaginable happiness and prosperity for you, provided it will help you to glorify God our Lord. And yet, when we reflect, these infirmities and other temporal privations are often seen to be from God's hand to help us to a better self-knowledge and to rid ourselves of the love of created things. They help us moreover to focus our thought on the brevity of this life, so as to prepare for the other which has no end. When I think that in these afflictions He visits those whom He loves, I can feel no sadness or pain, because I realize that a servant of God, through an illness, turns out to be something of a doctor for the direction and ordering of his life to God's glory and service.

You also speak of my forgiving you if you can no longer help me, since you have many obligations to meet and your resources are not sufficient for all. There is no reason for you to speak of forgiveness from me. It is I who should be afraid, for when I think of failing to do what God wishes me to do for all my benefactors, I begin to fear that His divine Justice will not forgive me, and all the more so, that I have received so much from you. Finally, since I am quite unable to fulfill my duties in this respect, my only refuge is to consider the merits I shall gain before the Divine Majesty, that is, with the help of His grace, which the same Lord will distribute to those to whom I am indebted, to each one according as he has helped me in His service, and especially to you, to whom I owe more than to anyone else I know in the world. As I recognize this debt, I hope that our Lord will come to my aid and help me to repay it. Be sure of this, that henceforth your affection for me which has been so solid and sincere will bring me as much spiritual joy and delight as if you sent me all the money in the world. Our Lord insists that we look to the giver, and love him more than his gift, and thus keep him ever before our eyes and in the most intimate thoughts of our heart.

You also suggest that I write, if I think it good, to our other sisters and benefactresses in Christ to ask help for the future. I would rather be guided in this by your judgment than by my own. Even though La Cepilla [1] offered in her letter and shows a desire to help me, I do not think for the present that I will write her for help in my studies. My reason is that there is no certainty of my remaining here for a whole year. And if I do God, I hope, will give me the light and judgment to do all for His greater service and always carry out His will and desire.

In the third letter, you speak of the enmities, the intrigues, the untruths which have been circulated about you. I am not at all surprised at this, not even if it were worse than it is. For just as soon as you determined to bend every effort to secure the praise, honor and service of God our Lord, you declared war against the world, and raised your standard in its face, and got ready to reject what is lofty by embracing what is lowly, to accept indifferently honor and dishonor, riches and poverty, affection and hatred, welcome and repulse, in a word, the glory of the world or all the wrongs it could inflict upon you. We cannot be much afraid of the reproaches of this life when they are confined to words, for all the words in the world will never hurt a hair of our heads.

As to words of double meaning, even when they are vile and hurtful, they will give neither pain nor satisfaction, except in so far as they are wilfully admitted. But if we wish absolutely to live in honor and to be held in esteem by our neighbors, we can never be solidly rooted in God our Lord, and it will be impossible for us to remain unscathed when we meet with affronts. Thus, the satisfaction I once took in the thought of the insults the world offered you was balanced by the pain I felt at the thought of your having to seek a remedy against this pain and suffering. May it please the Mother of God to hear my prayer for you, which is that you may meet with even greater affronts, so that you may have the occasion of greater merit, provided that you can accept them with patience and constancy and without sin on the part of others, remembering the greater insults which Christ our Lord suffered for us. If we find that we are without this patience, we have all the more reason to complain, not so much of those who hurt us, as of our own weakness and sensuality and our failure to be mortified and dead, as we should be, to the things of the world. For these people make it possible for us to gain a more precious treasure than any that one can win in this life, and greater riches than anyone can amass in this world. . . .

Thus, I would rather fix my attention on one fault that I had committed than on all the evil that might be said of me.

May the Most Holy Trinity grant you in all your trials and in everything else in which you can serve God all the grace that I desire for myself, and may no more be given to me than I desire for you.

Please remember me most sincerely to Master Roser, and to any who you think will be pleased to hear from me.

Paris, November 10, 1532.

Yours poor in goodness,

Iñigo

To Martin Garcia de Oñaz

Ignatius expresses his approval of his brother Martin's plans of sending his nephew to Paris to study. He then goes on to explain why he did not write at first, but does so now. He speaks of Christian charity and the order to be followed in charity, and encourages Martin to merit the goods of eternity by a proper use of those of time.

Paris, June 1532

IHS

May the grace and love of Christ our Lord be ever with us.

Your letter brought me great satisfaction in the service and love of the Divine Majesty because of the news it gives me of your daughter and the plans you have for your son. May the Divine Majesty be pleased with all our intentions and order them to His praise and service, and allow you to persevere in these good purposes and prosper them when you so direct them. If you have no better plan, I do not think that you will make any mistake in having him take theology rather than canon law, for theology is a field in which he will find it easier to amass the riches that do not fail, and which will give you added comfort in your old age. Nor do I think that you will find anywhere in Europe greater advantages than here at Paris. I should judge that if you allow him fifty ducats a year, he will be able to meet all expenses, tutor's fees and other charges. He will be in a foreign land, with different ways and a colder climate, and I am sure that you would not want him to suffer any need that might interfere with his studies; so it seems to me. Even from the point of view of expense, I am sure that he will find it cheaper, as he will be able to accomplish here in four years what it would take him six to do elsewhere, even more, I think I can say without straying from the truth. If you agree with me and send him here, it would be good to see that he arrives a week before the feast of St. Remy, the first of October next, as the courses in philosophy begin then. If he is well grounded in grammar he could begin his philosophy by that date. Should he come a little late, he will have to wait a whole year until the feast of St. Remy, when the course will begin over again.

I will do all I can to give him a start in his studies, and see that he applies himself and keeps away from bad company. You write: "If you decide that he is to live where you are, please let me know what it will cost a year. If you can be of any help to me in this matter of expense, I will see that you are repaid when opportunity offers." I believe that I understand the literal meaning of your words, if there has been no slip of the pen. You mean that you will appreciate it if your son studies here, and that I should do all I can to relieve you of all expense. I do not know what makes you say that, or what you mean by it. If it serves any purpose, make your meaning clear. As far as justice and reason are concerned, I do not think that God will permit me to be wanting, since all I seek is His most holy service, your comfort in Him, and your son's progress, in the event you make up your mind to send him here.

You say that you are delighted to see that I have taken to writing again after so long a period of neglect. Don't be surprised. A man with a serious wound begins by applying one ointment, and then in the course of its healing another,

and at the end still another. Thus, in the beginning of my
way, one kind of remedy was necessary, a little later a different one does me no harm. If I saw that it did I would
not look for a second or a third. It is not strange that I
should have had this experience, seeing that St. Paul said,
shortly after his conversion: "There was given me a sting
of my flesh, an angel of Satan to buffet me" (2 Cor. 12:7);
and elsewhere, "I see another law in my members, fighting
against the law of my mind" (Rom. 7:23); "the flesh lust-
ing against the spirit and the spirit against the flesh" (Gal.
5:17). And so great was the rebellion in his soul that he
went so far as to say, "For the good which I will I do not,
but the evil which I will not, that I do" (Rom. 7:19); "for
that which I work I understand not" (Rom. 7:15). Later,
on another occasion, "For I am sure that neither life nor
death, nor angels, nor things present, nor things to come,
nor any other creature shall be able to separate me from the
love of our Lord Jesus Christ" (Rom. 8:38-39). At the beginning of my way I was very much like him. Throughout
my life and at its end, may it please the Supreme Goodness
not to deny me His abundant and most holy grace that I
may be like all who are His true servants, and imitate and
serve them. I would ask Him even to take away my life
rather than that I should grieve Him in anything, or grow
slack in His service and praise.

But to come to the point. I would have written you more
frequently during the last five or six years but for two reasons. The first, my studies and my constant association with
others, which, however, had nothing to do with temporal interests. The second was that I did not have sufficient reason
for thinking that my letters would redound to the praise and
service of God our Lord, or so to comfort my kindred according to the flesh as to make us kindred according to the
spirit, and to help us both in the things that last forever.
The truth is I can love a person in this life only so far as

he strives to advance in the service and praise of God our Lord; for he who loves anything for itself, and not for God, does not love God with his whole heart. If two persons serve God equally, and one of them is a relative of mine, God wishes us to cherish a greater affection for our natural father than for another. He would have us prefer a benefactor and a relative to one who is neither; a friend and acquaintance to one who is unknown to us. For this reason, we revere, honor and love the Apostles more than we do the other saints, since they loved God our Lord more perfectly and served Him more faithfully. For charity, without which no one can attain eternal life, is the love with which we love God our Lord for Himself and everything else for Him. And we must also praise God in His saints, as the psalmist teaches us (Ps. 150:1).

I have a great desire, a very great desire indeed, if I may say so, to see a true and intense love of God grow in you, my relatives and friends, so that you will bend all your efforts to the praise and service of God. Doing this you make it possible for me to love you and serve you ever more and more, because in this service of the servants of my Lord there is for me both victory and glory. It is with this solid love and honest desire that I speak, write and advise you just as I should honestly wish and desire you to advise, urge and correct me in terms of sincere humility without any thought of worldly or profane glory. It is none of my business to condemn a man who in this life lies awake with plans for adding to his buildings, his income, his estate in the hope of leaving behind him a great name and reputation. But neither can I praise him, for, according to St. Paul, we ought to use the things of this world as though we used them not, and own them as though we owned them not, because the fashion of this world passes and in a moment is gone (1 Cor. 7:29-31). God grant that it may be so.

If any of these truths have in the past made any impression on you, or if they do so now, I beg of you by God's reverence and love, to make every effort to win honor in heaven, fame and renown before the Lord Who is going to be our Judge. For if He has given you an abundance of this world's goods, it is to help you earn those of heaven by giving a good example and sound teaching to your sons, servants and relatives. Converse spiritually with some, impose a proper punishment on others, without anger or harshness. Share with some the influence of your family, and help others with money and goods. Deal with an open hand with poor orphans and the needy. The man with whom our Lord has been so generous should not be close. One day we shall find in heaven as much repose and delight as we have dispensed in this life, and since you can do so much where you are, I beg of you again and again, by the love of our Lord Jesus Christ, to make every effort not only to give this matter some thought, but to put it into practice, because for those who love, nothing is hard, especially when done for the love of our Lord Jesus Christ.

I have written at this great length to answer once for all the detailed questions set down in your letter and to make you fully acquainted with the situation.

To the lady of the house, and all the family together, with all those who you think will be glad to hear from me, my sincerest regards in the Lord Who must judge us. Begging Him by His infinite and perfect Goodness to give us the grace to know his most holy will and the strength most perfectly to fulfil it, I remain, . . .

I received your letter on the twentieth of this month of June, and as you were very urgent about an answer, I am writing this and two copies, in the hope that what you decide in our Lord may not be without effect. If this letter reaches you in time, it will be all the better if your son arrives three weeks in advance of the feast of St. Remy, or even earlier, if possible, as he would then be able to make some preparation before beginning the course. A nephew of the Archbishop of Seville wishes to do this, having registered here in the college of St. Barbara for philosophy this coming feast of St. Remy. They could both take advantage of this introduction, as there will be no lack of opportunity. May the perfect Goodness be pleased to ordain all to His holy service and continued praise.

Poor in goodness,

Yñigo

To Sister Teresa Rejadella

Ignatius consoles her on the occasion of the death of her sister, Louise, by assuring her that her sister is in heaven. He settles some doubts concerning the Rules and the habit of the Order to which Teresa belongs, and goes on to explain the principles concerning daily communion. He shows that it is not forbidden either by the Church or the theologians, and tells her that if the love of God grows in her soul with the practice, it will not only be lawful but even preferable to receive daily.

Rome, November 15, 1543

IHS

May the perfect grace and love of Christ our Lord continue to help and favor us always.

1   I have heard that it was God's will to remove your sister Louise, and ours in our Lord, from the trials of this present life. I have every reason to believe with certainty that she is in a better life, a glorious and eternal life, where I hope she will favor and reward us with holy usury, seeing that we have not forgotten her in our own poor and unworthy prayers. Were I therefore to attempt to console you at length, I should feel that I were doing you wrong, as I must judge that you conform yourself as you should to the perfect and everlasting providence of God, which is entirely concerned with our greater glory.

2   As to the habit and observance of rule: ² if you have a judgment in your favor, or at least since you have a confirmation from the Apostolic See, you should have no doubts, as it is certain that you are in conformity with the service and the will of God. For a rule of any saint can oblige under pain of sin only in so far as it is approved by the Vicar of Christ our Lord, or by someone else who speaks with his authority. Consequently, the Rule of St. Benedict, of St. Francis, of St. Jerome, has no force of itself to oblige under pain of sin, but can do so only when it has the confirmation and authorization of the Apostolic See, because of the divine efficacy which it can impart to such a Rule.

3   As to daily communion, we should recall that in the early Church everybody received daily, and that up to this time there has been no written ordinance of Holy Mother Church, nor objection by either positive or scholastic theologians against anyone receiving daily communion should his devotion move him thereto. It is true that St. Augustine said that he would neither praise nor blame daily communion, but he did, on the other hand, exhort everyone to receive on Sundays.³ Further on, speaking of the most sacred Body of Christ our Lord, he says: "This bread is our daily bread. So live, therefore, as to be able to receive it daily." Now, this being true, even if the indications are not so good, or the inclinations of the soul so wholesome, the witness on which we can always rely is that of our own conscience. What I mean is this. After all, it is lawful for you in the Lord if, apart from evident mortal sins or what you judge to be such, you think that your soul derives help and is inflamed with love for our Creator and Lord, and you receive with this intention, finding from experience that this spiritual food soothes, supports, settles and preserves you for His greater service, praise and glory, you may without doubt receive daily, in fact, it would be better for you to do so.⁴

On this point and on some others I have spoken to Araoz,

who will deliver this letter. Referring you to him in everything in our Lord, I close, praying God our Lord by His
infinite kindness to guide you and govern you in all things
through His infinite and supreme Goodness.

Rome, November 15, 1543.

Poor in goodness,
Iñigo

To a Man Who Was Tempted

The recipient of this letter is unknown. He apparently had some connection with the community in Padua. He wished to return to his homeland or remain in the house at Padua, without however being a member of the community. This St. Ignatius refused to permit. In words that breathe of affection for the tempted man, Ignatius persuades him to leave the Society's house, but not to return to his home. He should devote himself to good works and take up some study at Padua, and not omit proper recreation.

November 28, 1544

Jhus

May the perfect grace of Christ our Lord ever be our protection and support.

I could not at all fail in the affection my heart feels for you, and so I will briefly answer your letter and that of Master Laynez, as God grants me understanding.

First, with regard to your going back home and living there, I do not think that anything could be worse for you; because, as past experience proves, it is the last thing you should think of, as I have explained at length in other letters.

Secondly, I do not think that I could approve of your remaining in the house with Ours, nor can I feel satisfied that it would be a good thing; partly, because you would not

87

find the fruit you are looking for and which you have every right to expect, and partly because of the disappointment both Ours and you would feel at their inability to help you in body and soul as they desire. All things considered, I always thought that it would be safer in our Lord, and better for all concerned, if you took lodging apart from Ours in Padua, with some good companions, paying what you would expect to pay at home, and try that out for a year. You should go to confession frequently and have a talk with some of Ours several times a week. For the rest, you could attend several lectures, but with the purpose rather of strengthening and clearing your mind than of acquiring academic learning for the sake of others. See that your associations are pleasant, and take some innocent recreation that will leave the soul unsullied, for it is better to keep the soul unsullied than to be made lord of all creation. By means of these interior consolations and the spiritual relish they will give you, you will attain to that peace and repose of conscience, and then, as your strength of body and soul allows, you can better give yourself to study for the sake of others and be sure of better results. But above all, I beg of you for the love and reverence of God our Lord to remember the past, and reflect not lightly but seriously that the earth is only earth.

May God in His infinite and perfect Goodness be pleased to give us His perfect grace, so that we may know His most holy will and entirely fulfil it.

Rome, November 28, 1544.

To Francis Borgia, Duke of Gandia

Ignatius exalts the saintly Duke and humbling himself gives him admirable direction on the perfect union of man with God, the value of God's grace, the obstacles which souls oppose to it, and the fruit of frequent communion. He ends with a courteous plea for the College of Gandia.

Rome, end of 1545

My lord in our Lord.

May the perfect love and everlasting favor of our Lord visit and abide with your Lordship.

On the last of October I received your letter of July 24th, written in your own hand. It has given me more than a little joy in our Lord to learn from it of matters that are drawn rather from an interior experience than from anything external; an experience which our Lord in His infinite Goodness usually gives to those souls who render themselves entirely to Him as the beginning, middle and end of all our good. May His holy Name be praised and exalted in all and by all creatures, which are created and ordained to an end that is so just and proper.

But to come to particulars, I will take some of the points about which you write as they come to mind. You ask that I be not unmindful of you in my prayers and that I give you the consolation of writing you. I have remembered you daily in my prayers and do still, and I hope in our Lord that if they win you any favor it will be entirely from on high, descending from His infinite Goodness. Were I to consider only God's eternal and perfect liberality, and the devotion and holy purpose of your Lordship, I should be convinced that in seeing you so spiritually minded I have not failed you in the past. As to the consolation of my letters, of which your Lordship speaks, I find it easy to persuade myself that you will find consolation not only in these letters, but in all things, seeing that when men abandon themselves to belong to their Creator they gain an intimate knowledge, which is full of consolation, of how our eternal good exists throughout all creation, giving each creature existence and preserving it in His own infinite Being and presence. These considerations, I am sure, and many others will provide you with an abundance of consolation. For we know that all creatures are at the service of those who love God entirely and that they help them to even greater merit and joy and union through an intense charity for their Creator and Lord, despite the fact that the creature often opposes obstacles, as your Lordship so well observes, to the effects our Lord wishes to produce in the soul.

Not only does man set up these obstacles before receiving these graces, gifts and consolations of the Holy Spirit, but even after he has received them; graces of consolation in which all darkness and restless worry are removed from the soul, and the soul itself adorned with the spiritual blessings that bring it contentment and cause it to fall in love with the things that continue in endless glory. Even then we allow ourselves to be distracted with thoughts about trifles, without knowing how to keep so heavenly a blessing. In fact, we set up obstacles before our Lord lavishes His graces upon us and after He has done so, with the result that we fail to retain them.

Your Lordship mentions such obstacles, more to lower yourself in our Lord and to exalt us who wish to abase ourselves, when you say, relying from what you hear from Araoz in Portugal, that this Society places no obstacles to what our Lord desires to work in it. For my part, I am convinced that I am nothing but obstacle, both before and after, because I can thus attribute nothing to myself which has any appearance of good. I am convinced of this one thing, with due regard for the opinion of others who are better informed, that there are very few in this world, nay, I will go further and say that there is no one who during this mortal life can properly judge how far he is an obstacle and to what extent he resists the workings of God's grace in his soul. I am quite satisfied that the more advanced and experienced and perfect one is in humility and charity, the more one will be aware, even in the most insignificant thoughts, of the slightest things that stand in his way and oppose him, even though they may appear to be of little or no importance. And yet, we shall never, in this life at least, have a full knowledge of our obstacles and faults, as the Prophet asks to be freed from the faults he knows not,[5] and St. Paul,[6] admitting that he is ignorant of them, adds that he is not for that reason justified.

As I understand from your letters, our Lord Who is to be my Judge, makes you, in His infinite Mercy, a scholar in so holy a school. This is a fact which you cannot deny, if you look into your own soul. It is my earnest wish in our Lord that you do your very best to recruit as many fellow scholars as possible, beginning with the members of your own household (to whom we are most obligated), and bring them by the surest and most direct way to His Divine Majesty. Now, since this way is none other than Christ our Lord, as He Himself says,[7] I give many thanks to His divine Goodness because your Lordship approaches the altar frequently to receive Him, according to what I have heard here. Besides the many rich graces which the soul gains in the reception of her Creator and Lord, there is one that is particularly outstanding, since it is one that will not permit a man to remain long and obstinately in sin. But as soon as one falls into what we call little sins—if any can be called little when the object [8] is the infinite and Supreme Good—He raises him up again with renewed and increased strength and a firmer determination to serve his Creator and Lord.

As you advance in this way with the help of God's grace, and make use of the gifts which the Divine Majesty has mercifully bestowed upon you to win your brethren and your neighbors, you make me your debtor, without any merit on my part, for the desire I feel to imitate your Lordship.

You write that you desire to have some share in the business affairs which weigh so heavily upon me here in the governing of our Society, a task which has been laid upon me by God's will, or permitted by His eternal Goodness as a punishment for my great and fearful sins. I beg your Lordship by the love and reverence of God our Lord to help me with your prayers, and also to be good enough to help me by taking charge of the government and seeing to the completion of a house or college that is desired in Gandia for the scholastics of the Society,[9] which is not only your Lordship's wish, but also the Lady Duchess's [10] and the Lady Juana's,[11] her sister. It was at the request of your Lordship, which for us is a command, that these scholastics were received, and we hope that you will continue to help the establishment with your favor and protection in our Lord, as you may judge to be to His greater glory. We are now all the more delighted in the Divine Goodness that a relative of the Lady Duchess [12] has entered, as your Lordship writes me, and that her Ladyship is so pleased. I beg your Lordship to recommend me to the favor and prayers of her Ladyship and to those of the Lady Juana. In closing, I ask the Divine Majesty to grant us the fulness of His grace, so that we may know His holy will and perfectly fulfil it.

Rome, end of 1545.

Ignatio

To Doimus Nascius[13]

An answer to a religious who threatened to burn every Jesuit he found between Perpignan and Seville.[14]

Rome, August 10, 1546

Jhs

Master Doimus.

Tell Father Barbaran that as he says he will have burned all of Ours to be found between Perpignan and Seville, it is also my desire that both he and all his friends and acquaintances, not only between Perpignan and Seville, but throughout the whole world, should be enkindled and inflamed by the Holy Spirit, and that by thus reaching a high degree of perfection, they will be distinguished in the glory of His Divine Majesty.

Tell him also that a trial is in progress before their Lordships, the Governor and the Vicar of His Holiness, in which our fortunes are at stake, and that they are about to pass judgment. If he has anything against us, I invite him to come and submit his proofs before the above mentioned judges. Should the verdict go against us, I should rejoice the more if I alone were to suffer, and thus save all those between Perpignan and Seville from being burned.

Rome, from our Lady of the Wayside, August 10, 1546.

Iñigo

To St. Francis Borgia

The Duke of Gandia was by this time a professed member of the Society of Jesus. By virtue of a papal brief, he continued with the administration of his estates, and in his palace led the life of a saint. In one of his letters to the Founder of the Society, he had given his opinion on his own exercises of prayer and penance. In the following letter St. Ignatius gives him rules that are full of wisdom to help him arrive at the proper mean in these exercises.

Rome, September 20, 1548

IHS

May the perfect grace and everlasting love of Christ our Lord be always in our favor and help.

When I hear how harmoniously you have reconciled your spiritual and temporal interests and directed them to your spiritual progress, I find fresh reason, I assure you, for rejoicing in our Lord, and while giving thanks to His Eternal Majesty I can attribute my joy only to His Divine Goodness, which is the source of all our blessings. And yet, I realize in our Lord that at one time we may be in need of certain exercises, spiritual as well as physical, and at another time we will need others: because those which for a season have proved profitable may cease to be so later, I will tell you what I think in His Divine Majesty on this subject, since your Lordship has asked for my views.

First. I should think that the time devoted to these exercises, both interior and exterior, should be reduced by half. We ought to increase these exercises, both interior and exterior, when our thoughts arise from ourselves, or are suggested by our enemy, and lead us to fix our attention on objects that are distracting, frivolous or forbidden, if we wish to prevent the will from taking any satisfaction in them or yielding any consent. I say that as a rule we ought to increase these exercises, both interior and exterior, the more these thoughts are multiplied, in order to conquer them, keeping in mind the character of the individual and the varying nature of the thoughts and temptations, and being careful to measure the exercises to the capacity of the individual. Contrariwise, when these thoughts lose their strength and cease, their place will be taken by holy thoughts and inspirations, and to these we must give the utmost welcome by opening to them all the doors of the soul. Consequently there will be no further need of so many weapons to overthrow the enemy.

From what I can judge of your Lordship in our Lord, it would be better if you were to devote to study about half the time that you now give to these exercises. In the future learning will always be very necessary, or certainly useful, and not only that which is infused, but that also which is acquired by study. Some of your time should be given to the administration of your estates and to spiritual conversation. Try to keep your soul always in peace and quiet, always ready for whatever our Lord may wish to work in you. It is certainly a more lofty virtue of the soul, and a greater grace, to be able to enjoy the Lord in different duties and places than in one only. We should, in the divine Goodness, make a great effort to attain this.

Secondly. As to fasts and abstinences, I would advise you to be careful and strengthen your stomach for our Lord, and your other physical powers, rather than weaken them. My reason is that, in the first place, when a soul is so disposed to lose its own life rather than offend God's Majesty by even the slightest deliberate sin, and is moreover comparatively free from the temptations of the world, the flesh and the devil (a condition of soul which I am sure your Lordship by God's grace enjoys), I should like very much to see your Lordship imprint in your soul the truth that as both body and soul are a gift from your Creator and Lord, you should give Him a good account of both. To do this you must not allow your body to grow weak, for if you do, the interior man will no longer be able to function properly. Therefore, although I once highly praised fasting and abstinence even from so many ordinary foods, and for a certain period was pleased with this program, I cannot praise it for the future, when I see that the stomach, because of these fasts and abstinences, cannot function naturally or digest any of the ordinary meats or other items of diet which contribute to the proper maintenance of the body. I should rather have you seek every means of strengthening the body. Eat, therefore, whatever food is allowed and as often as you find it convenient. But it should be done without offence to the neighbor. We should love the body in so far as it is obedient and helpful to the soul, since the soul with the body's help and service is better disposed for the service and praise of our Creator and Lord.

Thirdly. Concerning the ill treatment of the body for our Lord's sake, I would say, avoid anything that would cause the shedding even of a drop of blood. If His Divine Majesty has given you the grace for this and for all that I have mentioned (it is my conviction that He has), it would be better for the future without reasons or arguments, to drop this penance, and instead of trying to draw blood, seek more immediately the Lord of all, or what comes to the same thing, seek His most holy gifts, such as the gift of tears. This could be 1) because of our own sins or the sins of others; or 2) while contemplating the mysteries of the life of Christ, either here on earth or in heaven; or 3) from a loving consideration of the Three Divine Persons. Thus, the higher our thoughts soar the greater will be their worth. The third is more perfect in itself than the second, and the second than the first. But, for a given person that level will be much better on which our Lord communicates more of Himself in His holy graces and spiritual gifts, because He sees and knows what is best for you. Like one who knows all He points out the way to you. On our part, with the help of His grace, we will learn by making trial of many methods, so that we may advance along the way that stands out clearest, which will be for us the happiest and most blessed in this life, leading us directly by ordered paths to that other everlasting life, after having united us in a close embrace with His most holy gifts.

By these gifts I understand those that are beyond the reach of our own powers, which we cannot attain at will, since they are rather a pure gift of Him Who bestows them and Who alone can give every good. These gifts, with His Divine Majesty as their end, are faith, hope and charity, joy and spiritual repose, tears, intense consolation, elevation of mind, divine impressions and illuminations together with all other spiritual relish and understanding which have these gifts as their objects, such as a humble reverence for our holy Mother the Church, her rulers and teachers. Any of these holy gifts should be preferred to exterior and visible manifestations which are good only when they have one or other of these higher gifts as their object. I do not mean to say that we should seek them merely for the satisfaction or pleasure they give us. We know, however, that without them all our thoughts, words and actions are of themselves tainted, cold, disordered, while with them they become clear and warm and upright for God's greater service. It is for this reason that we should desire these gifts, or some of them, and spiritual graces; that is, in so far as they are a help to us, to God's greater glory. Thus, when the body falls ill because of excessive effort, it is the most reasonable thing to seek these gifts by acts of the understanding and other more moderate exercises. For it is not the soul alone that should be healthy. If the mind is healthy in a healthy body, all will be healthy and much better prepared to give God greater service.

As to how you should act in individual cases, I do not think it wise in the Lord to speak in detail. It is my hope that the same Divine Spirit Who has hitherto guided your Lordship will continue to guide you and rule you in the future, to the greater glory of His Divine Majesty.

Rome, September 20, 1548.

To Father Antonio Brandão

The Portuguese, Antonio Brandão, already ordained, had accompanied Simon Rodrigues on a journey from Portugal to Rome. He laid before Polanco a list of fifteen questions to be submitted to Ignatius. We offer both questions and answers, as they all deal with some very practical aspects of the spiritual life, the answers being very revealing with regard to the direction of St. Ignatius for the scholastics of the Society.

In the houses of study of the Society, study is one of the obligations of a state of life. Instead of increasing by rule the exercises of piety, one should get accustomed to seeking God in all things, to offering Him one's studies and intellectual labors, and to nourishing the holy desire of helping souls. In the matter of confession, one ought to examine the slightest imperfections should the devil attempt to cause one to lean towards laxity. If one is at peace with God, the confession should be brief without going into details, but with an effort to arouse sorrow for the offense. Make use of sacramentals. Authority and affection are a great help in the matter of fraternal correction, but in no case should one resort to rudeness in making one's observations.

June 1, 1551

IHS

Instructions which are given by our Father Ignatius, or by his direction, to those who live away from Rome, and other points worthy of notice which should not be forgotten.

99

For Portugal.

A scholastic of the Society (Father Brandão) wishes to have our Father's direction on the following points:

1. How much time should be given to prayer by a scholastic still at his studies, and how much time should he spend conversing with his brethren, supposing that the Rector sets no limits to these occupations?

2. Should Mass be said daily, or only on certain days even when it seems an obstacle to study?

3. After finishing philosophy should one give more time to speculative or to moral theology on the supposition that one does not give oneself entirely to both subjects in the colleges?

4. What is to be done when one finds oneself entertaining an inordinate ambition for learning?

5. Should one offer oneself to the superior before being asked to do a certain work, or leave the whole matter in his hands?

6. What method of meditation that is more in keeping with our vocation should be followed?

7. In confession, should one descend to particular imperfections, or be satisfied with mentioning the more general faults, so as to be brief?

8. If the confession is made to a member of the community and the confessor questions the penitent, even though there is no question of sin, in what instance should he ask the penitent's permission to inform the superior on the subject-matter of the confession?

9. What attitude should one take in treating with the superior concerning the difficulties of others? Should he make a complete revelation of them, even though some of them have ceased to be troublesome?

10. Should one correct any imperfection that is noticed in a member of the Society, or should it be allowed to pass, allowing the individual to be deceived into thinking it is no imperfection?

11. If before God one believes that the superior, the Rector, for instance, is not right in a certain matter, should the Provincial be informed, and thus of other subordinate superiors, or should one close one's eyes?

12. What rule should be followed in writing either to externs or to Ours, when there is no real need or command of obedience, but merely for motives of charity?

13. In dealing with externs or Ours should they use language which might appear to them to be mere civility, or should they avoid all forms of flattery?

14. What should one do about giving information concerning one of the Society, and how should it be done?

15. Or would it be lawful to counsel an extern, or one of the house without vows, to take vows?

What should they do about using or not using a privilege of the Society in dealing with a penitent?

The first question has two parts, and the answer to the first part is to remember that the purpose of a scholastic at his studies in the college is to learn, to acquire that knowledge with which he can serve God's greater glory and be of help to his neighbor. This is a task that demands all that a man has, and he will not give himself completely to his studies if he also gives a large amount of time to prayer. Hence, it will be sufficient if scholastics who are not priests (supposing no interior disturbance or exceptional devotion), give one hour to prayer over and above the Mass. During Mass the scholastic should make a short meditation while the priest is at the secret parts. But at the hour of prayer he would ordinarily recite the Hours of Our Lady, or some other prayer, or meditate, should the Rector judge that to be better. If the scholastic is a priest, it will be enough for him to say his office, celebrate Mass and make the examens. Should his devotion move him he could add another half-hour.

The second part of the question will be answered if we consider the purpose of conversing with others, which is to influence for good him with whom we converse. This edification is hindered by excess in either direction, and we should therefore avoid extremes and try to hold a middle course.

With respect to the last clause of this question, our Reverend Father made some remarks on the great esteem we should have for obedience. Some saints have excellences that are wanting in others, and the same is true of religious Orders. It was his desire, therefore, that in the Society there be an excellence which would put it on a footing with any other religious Orders, even if they had excellences which we could not aspire to equal, although we might well make the attempt in some things, poverty, for instance. But our Reverend Father wished that our excellence be obedience, as we had a greater obligation to excel in it because of the extra vow of obedience which the fathers had to the Sovereign Pontiff, which does away with every excuse we might have for not carrying out an order of obedience. And he also said that this obedience could not be perfect, unless the understanding of the subject was in complete conformity with the understanding of the superior. Without this conformity life would be a continual purgatory, and with little hope of stability.

To the second question our Reverend Father answered that, considering the purpose one of Ours should have in his studies, he could be satisfied with two Masses a week, over and above Sundays and feast days, supposing that none of these three reasons persuaded otherwise, 1) obedience, 2) the common good, 3) exceptional devotion.

To the third question, preference should be given to speculative theology, because after finishing with the colleges one has to devote oneself to moral theology, as that is necessary for conferences and other occasions, and speculative theology is proper to the schools where fundamental truths are taken for study.

The fourth question will be answered along with the sixth.

The fifth: it would be good once for all to offer oneself to the superior for him to dispose of one to the greater glory of God our Lord, leaving all care of self to him as holding the place of Christ our Lord on earth, seldom making any representation, unless something occurs which might especially require it.

The sixth. Considering the end of our studies, the scholastics can hardly give themselves to prolonged meditations. Over and above the spiritual exercises assigned for their perfection, namely, daily Mass, an hour for vocal prayer and examen of conscience, weekly confession and communion, they should practice the seeking of God's presence in all things, in their conversations, their walks, in all that they see, taste, hear, understand, in all their actions, since His Divine Majesty is truly in all things by His presence, power and essence. This kind of meditation which finds God our Lord in all things is easier than raising oneself to the consideration of divine truths which are more abstract and which demand something of an effort if we are to keep our attention on them. But this method is an excellent exercise to prepare us for great visitations of our Lord, even in prayers that are rather short. Besides this, the scholastics can frequently offer to God our Lord their studies and the efforts they demand, seeing that they have undertaken them for His love to the sacrifice of their personal tastes, so that to some extent at least we may be of service to His Divine Majesty and of help to the souls for whom He died. We can also make these exercises the matter of our examen.

To these exercises may be added that of preaching in the colleges. After the example of a good life, one of the most efficient means of helping the neighbor and one which is especially in order in the Society is preaching. Our Reverend

Father was of the opinion that no little fruit could be gathered if the scholastics were exercised in preaching. He thought they should preach on Sundays, on subjects of their own choosing, and as an exercise that entailed no loss of time, two or three of them could at supper recite the formula of the tones which they had been taught, using at first the formula that is in use here at Rome. As the possibilities of this are exhausted, another could easily be taken which could be developed in keeping with local customs. The advantages of this exercise are very great, but for brevity's sake we omit them here.

The seventh deals with confession. To avoid any mistake, we should notice from which side the enemy launches his attack and tries to make us offend our Lord. If he aims at getting us to commit mortal sins easily, the penitent should weigh well even the least imperfections which lead to that sin, and confess them. If he finds himself drawn to doubts and perplexities, making sin out of what is not sin, he should not descend into minute details, but mention only his venial sins, and of these only the more important. If by God's grace the soul is at peace with God our Lord, let him confess his sins briefly without going into detail. He should try to feel confusion for them in God's presence, considering that He Who is offended is Infinite, which imparts a kind of infinity to the sin. But by the sovereign Goodness of God our Lord they are venial and are forgiven [15] by using a little holy water, striking one's breast, making an act of contrition, etc.

To the first part of the eighth, questions may and sometimes should be asked regarding certain venial faults, for they may be the means of revealing mortal sins, and help the penitent to a clear manifestation of his conscience, by which he may be further helped.

The second part of the eighth question. For greater clearness on this point, our Father insisted on the importance of the superior's being in touch with all that concerns his subjects, so that he could provide for each according to his needs. Thus, if he knows that one undergoes temptations of the flesh, he will not station him near the fire by assigning him, for example, to hear the confessions of women, etc. Nor will he entrust government to one who is lacking in obedience. To guard against anything like this happening, our Father usually reserves certain cases to himself, all mortal sins, for example, and vehement temptations against the Institute, the superior, and other forms of instability. Keeping this in mind, the confessor, according to the circumstances of each case, may discreetly ask leave to make a manifestation to the Superior. There is reason to believe that a troubled conscience will be helped more in the Lord in this way than in any other.

The ninth. The answer to the ninth may be surmised from the preceding, and it is that the superior should be wholly informed about everything, even of things past, always taking for granted one's good will, and with every precaution for the due observance of charity towards the neighbor.

The first part of the tenth concerns the correction of another. For this to be successful it will help much if the corrector has some authority, or acts with great affection, an affection that can be recognized. If either of these qualities is absent the correction will fail, that is, there will be no amendment. For this reason it would not be proper for everybody to undertake such correction. But in whatever manner it is done, and if one is reasonably certain that it will be well taken, one's admonition should not be too forthright, but toned down and presented without offense; because one sin leads to another, and it is quite possible that once committed, it will not dispose the sinner to accept even a well intentioned correction in the right spirit.

To the second part of the tenth, as to whether one should be left under the false impression that there is no imperfection, our Reverend Father says that it might be better for the person's progress to do so; and that the more one attends to the faults of others the less he will see of his own, and thus make less progress himself. But if one is really advancing, with his passions well under control and in good order, with our Lord expanding his heart so that he is a help to others as well as to himself, such a one may correct him who is in error provided the manner suggested in the eleventh number be followed.

As an answer to the eleventh question, our Father recounted what he said to the six who were together after making their profession, namely, that they could help him to perfection in two things: the first was their own perfection; the second was to call his attention to what they thought was contrary to this perfection in him. He wanted them to have recourse to prayer before they corrected him, and then if in the presence of God our Lord there was no change in their understanding and judgment, they were to tell him privately, a procedure which he himself follows now. Our Father said that it would be a great help to success in this matter if the superior entrusted this duty to some of his subjects, priests, for example, and others who were looked up to. He who wishes only to benefit himself would do well to close the eyes of his judgment. If anyone should have something to say, let him be careful first to place himself in the presence of our Lord, so as to know and to make up his mind what he ought to do. Secondly, he should find some acceptable manner of telling the delinquent, if he thinks that he will accept the correction. But if he thinks that he will not accept it, let him tell the superior. Our Father thought it would be a great advantage to have a syndic to make these things known to the Superior. Besides, he would have one or two act as vice-rectors, one subject to the other, to help the Rector, and with this arrangement the Rector would be much better able to be of greater help to one or the other, and would keep the affection of his subjects, as they would look upon him as a refuge if they thought themselves hardly dealt with by the vice-rectors.

Our Father gave an answer to the thirteenth which seems rather striking to me, namely, that in dealing with another, we should take a cue from the enemy who wishes to draw a man to evil. He goes in via the way of the man whom he wishes to tempt, but comes out his own way. We may thus adapt ourselves to the inclinations of the one with whom we are conversing, adapting ourselves in our Lord to everything, only to come out later with the good accomplished to which we had laid our hand.

Our Father made another remark as to how to free oneself from one whom there was no hope of helping. He suggests talking to him rather pointedly of hell, judgment, and such things. In that case, he would not return, or if he did, the chances are that he would feel himself touched in our Lord.

Finally, one should accommodate oneself to the character of him with whom one is dealing, whether he be phlegmatic, choleric, etc. But this should be done within limits.

The remaining questions depend more on the circumstances of individual cases, which in this instance are not given.

Rome, June 1, 1551.

To Father Manuel Godinho

The devout Father Manuel Godinho was much afflicted because he thought his office as treasurer of the College of Coimbra was an obstacle to his perfection in the religious life. It was in this sense that he must have written to St. Ignatius who in the following letter comforts and encourages him, reminding him of the supernatural end of the Society of Jesus, which end sanctifies exterior occupations that are undertaken through obedience.

January 31, 1552

May the perfect grace and everlasting love of Christ our Lord ever be in our favor and help.

I received your letter, dear brother in our Lord, and from it I learn of your arrival at San Fins with the brethren who are under your care there, and that everything was done with due edification.

Although the charge of temporal affairs seems to be and is distracting, I have no doubt that by your good and upright intention you turn everything you do to something spiritual for God's glory, and are thus very pleasing to His divine Goodness. For, the distractions which you accept for His greater service, in conformity with His divine will interpreted to you by obedience, can be not only the equivalent of the union and recollection of uninterrupted contemplation, bur even more acceptable to Him, proceeding as they do from

108

a more active and vigorous charity. May God our Creator and Lord deign to preserve this charity in your soul and in the souls of all. We rightly hold that any operation whatever in which charity is exercised to God's glory is very holy and suitable for us, and those activities even more so in which the infallible rule of obedience to our superiors has placed us. May He Who gave to Eliseus this twofold spirit, which you say is so necessary, give it to you in abundance. I will not be remiss in desiring and begging it of His Divine Majesty.

If looking only to God's glory, you still think that in God's service this office is unsuitable for you, confer with your superiors there, and they will do what is proper. Even here, as one who holds you very close to his heart, I will not fail to help you.

May Christ our Lord help us all with His bountiful grace, so that we may know His holy will and perfectly fulfil it.

Rome, January 31, 1552.

Yours in our Lord,
Ignatius

To the Province of Portugal

LETTER ON OBEDIENCE

In this famous Letter St. Ignatius has nothing that is completely new to say about obedience. His teaching is drawn entirely from tradition. He is repeatedly appealing to Scripture, the Fathers, the great monastic legislators. What Ignatius gives is emphasis. His teaching is not his own discovery, if we take discovery in the sense of invention. He may be said to have re-discovered for his own generation, and the generations to follow, the meaning, the weight, the dignity, the merit, the necessity of religious obedience, and to have brought these qualities to the attention of men and women who had for the most part lost sight of them. He did this concisely, coherently, cogently.

Certain explanations of religious obedience as set forth by St. Ignatius have been the occasion of controversy, not because they are inherently unacceptable, but because men have strangely misunderstood them and misinterpreted them. Attention will be called to them as they occur in the Letter.

Ignatius of Loyola sends greetings to his brethren of the Society of Jesus in Portugal, and wishes them the grace and everlasting love of Christ our Lord.

1 It is a cause of deep consolation to me, my dear brothers in Christ, to hear of the eager efforts you are making

in your striving after the highest perfection in virtue and in God's service. It is owing to His bounty that, having once called you to this way of life, He keeps you in it, as might be expected of His mercy, and guides you to that happy goal attained by those whom He has chosen.

2   Of course, I wish you to be perfect in all spiritual gifts and adornments. But it is especially in the virtue of obedience, as you have heard from me on other occasions, that I am anxious to see you signalize yourselves. I desire this, not only because of the rare and outstanding blessings connected with obedience, as may be seen from the many distinguished proofs and examples of it to be found in Holy Scripture, in both the Old and the New Testaments; but also because, as we read in St. Gregory: "Obedience is the only virtue which implants the other virtues in the heart, and preserves them after they have been so implanted." (*Moralium*, xxxv, 14, n. 28. PL 76, col. 765.) [16] With this virtue flourishing, the others will surely flourish and bring forth the fruits which I look for in your hearts, and which He requires Who by His saving obedience redeemed the human race which had been laid low and destroyed by the sin of disobedience, "becoming obedient unto death, even to the death of the cross." (Phil. 2:8.)

3   We may the more readily allow other religious orders to surpass us in the matter of fasting, watching, and other austerities in their manner of living, which all of them devoutly practice according to their respective Institutes. But in the purity and perfection of obedience and the surrender of our will and judgment, it is my warmest wish, beloved brethren, to see those who serve God in this Society signalize themselves. Indeed, the true and genuine sons of this Society should be recognized by this characteristic, that they never regard the individual himself whom they obey, but in him Christ our Lord for Whose sake they obey. For the superior is not to be obeyed because he is prudent, or kind, or divinely gifted in any other way, but for the sole reason that he holds

the place of God and exercises the authority of Him Who says, "He who hears you hears me, and he who despises you despises me." (Luke 10:16.) On the other hand, there should not be the least remissness in obedience to him, at least in so far as he is superior, because he happens to be less prudent or less experienced, since he is the representative of Him Whose wisdom cannot be mistaken, and Who will make good whatever is lacking in his representative, even though it be uprightness or other good qualities. Christ our Lord expressly declared this, when He said: "The scribes and Pharisees have sat on the chair of Moses," adding immediately, "all things, therefore, that they command you observe and do, but do not act according to their works." (Matt. 23:2, 3.)

4   For this reason it is my desire that you devote yourselves to an unremitting effort, and make it a practice to recognize Christ our Lord in any superior you may have, and with all devotion, reverence and obey the Divine Majesty in Him. This will seem the less surprising if you take note that St. Paul bids us obey our civil and pagan superiors as we would Christ, from Whom flows all legitimate authority. He writes to the Ephesians: "Slaves, obey your masters according to the flesh, with fear and trembling in the sincerity of your heart, as you would Christ: not serving to the eye as pleasers of men, but as slaves of Christ, doing the will of God from your heart, giving your service with good will as to the Lord and not to man. . . ." (Eph. 6:5-7.)

From this you yourselves can gather how a religious ought to regard one whom he has chosen not only as a superior, but expressly as Christ's representative, to be his guide and adviser: I mean, whether he should look upon him as a mere man, or as Christ's vicar.

5   Now, this is a point on which you should have a thorough understanding and which I am anxious to see solidly established in your minds, that the first and lowest degree of obedience is exceedingly imperfect, since it does not go be-

yond the bare execution of a command. In fact, it should not
be called obedience at all, unless it rises to the second degree
which makes the superior's will the subject's own, and not
only conforms it to the superior's will in the actual carrying
out of the command, but begets also a conformity of desires.
In this way what one wishes the other wishes and what one
rejects the other rejects. This is what we read in Holy Scripture: "Obedience is better than sacrifice" (1 Kings 15:22),
which is thus explained by St. Gregory: "In other sacrifices
the flesh of another is slain, but in obedience our own will is
sacrificed." (*Moralium*, xxxv, c. 14, n. 28. PL 76, col. 765.)
Precisely because this faculty of the mind is so precious, the
surrender of it to our Lord and Creator in obedience should
be held to be of great value.

6   In how great and perilous an error are they involved
who, not only in matters pertaining to flesh and blood, but
even in those which in other respects are holy and very spiritual, such as fasts, prayers, and other works of devotion, think
they are justified in withdrawing from the will and command
of their superior! Let them give heed to what Cassian wisely
observes in the *Conference of the Abbot Daniel:* "It is one
and the same kind of disobedience to break the command of
the superior, whether it be done from an interest in work or
a desire of ease, and as harmful to disregard the rules of the
monastery by going to sleep as by remaining awake. Finally,
it would be just as bad to fail to obey the command of the
Abbot, whether you did it to read or to sleep." (*Collationes*,
lib. IV, c. 20. PL 49, col. 608.) Martha's activity was holy
and holy was Magdalen's contemplation, and holy the peni-
tence and tears with which she bathed the feet of Christ our
Lord. But these things, it must be noted, were to be done in
Bethania, a name which the interpreters say means "House of
Obedience." According to St. Bernard, it would seem that our
Lord wished to point out to us that neither the zeal of good
actions, nor the repose of holy contemplation, nor the peni-

tent's tears would have been acceptable to Him anywhere but in Bethania. (*Sermo ad milites templi,* n. 13. PL 182, col. 939.)

7   As far as you can, therefore, my dear brothers, make a complete surrender of your wills. Dedicate as a free gift to your Creator, through His ministers, this liberty which He has bestowed upon you. Be sure of this, that it is no slight benefit to your free will to be allowed to restore it completely to Him from Whom you received it. In doing so, you not only do not lose it, but you even add to it and perfect it, when you conform your own will to that most certain norm of all righteousness, the will of God, which is interpreted for you by him who governs you in God's name.

8   Therefore, you must maintain a watchful guard against ever trying at any time to wrest the superior's will, which you should think of as God's, into agreement with your own. To do this would be not to conform your own will to God's, but to endeavor to rule God's by yours, and thus reverse the order of His Divine Wisdom. Great is the mistake of those whom self-love has blinded into thinking themselves obedient when they have by some stratagem bent the superior's will to their own wishes. Hear what St. Bernard, a man of exceptional experience in this matter, has to say: "Whoever either openly or covertly tries to have his spiritual father [17] enjoin him what he himself desires, deceives himself if he flatters himself into thinking that he is a true follower of obedience. For in this he does not obey his superior, but rather his superior obeys him." (*Sermo de tribus ordinibus Ecclesiae,* n. 4. PL 183, col. 636.)

If this is true, whoever wishes to attain the virtue of obedience must rise to this second degree, in which he not only fulfils the superior's commands, but even makes the superior's will his own, or rather strips himself of his own will to clothe himself with God's will as proposed to him by his superior.

9   But he who wishes to make an absolutely complete offering of himself must in addition to his will include his

understanding, which is the third and highest degree of obedience. The result will be that he not only identifies his will with that of the superior, but even his thought, and submits his own judgment to the superior's judgment, to the extent that a devout will can bend the understanding. For although this faculty is not endowed with the will's liberty and is naturally borne to assent to whatever is presented to it as true, nevertheless, in many instances, where the evidence of the known truth is not coercive, the intellect under the influence of the will may be inclined to this side rather than to that. In such circumstances everyone who makes profession of obedience must bow to the judgment of the superior.

As a matter of fact, obedience is a whole-burnt offering in which the entire man, without the slightest reserve, is offered in the fire of charity to his Creator and Lord by the hands of His ministers. It is at the same time a complete surrender in which a religious freely yields up his own rights for the purpose of being governed and possessed by Divine Providence through the agency of his superiors. It cannot be denied, therefore, that obedience includes not only the execution, which carries the superior's command into effect, and the will by doing so with a glad heart, but, in addition, it includes also the judgment, so that whatever the superior commands and thinks right ought to appear right and proper to the inferior, to the extent, as I have said, that the will has power to bend the understanding.

10   Would to God that this obedience of the understanding and judgment were as well understood by men and put into practice as it is pleasing to God and necessary for anyone leading the religious life! This necessity can be seen from a consideration of the heavenly bodies, where, if one is to have any effect upon another, or communicate its movement to it, this body must be subject and subordinate to the first. The same is true among men. If one is to be moved by another's authority, as is done in obedience, he who is in the position

of the inferior must accommodate himself to the commands and views of his superior, if the influence of the latter is to reach him and have any effect on him. Now, this subjection and subordination cannot exist unless there be a conformity of will and judgment between the subject and the superior.

11   Once more then, if we look to the end and purpose of obedience, it is just as possible for the intellect as for the will to be deceived as to what is good for us. And therefore, as the will is united with the superior's will to keep it from error, so the understanding must conform to the judgment of the superior to keep from being misled. "Lean not on thine own prudence," is the warning of Holy Scripture. (Prov. 3:5.)

Even in the temporal affairs of life, the wise think that the truly prudent man should have little confidence in his own prudence, especially when personal interests are at stake, in which men who are not easy in mind can hardly ever be good judges. Now, if in our own personal affairs we ought to think more of the judgment and advice of another, even when he is not our superior, how much more should we think of that judgment and advice when he is our superior, a man to whom we have surrendered ourselves to be ruled as to God's representative and the interpreter of His holy will!

Certain it is that in men and matters spiritual even greater caution is necessary, seeing that there is greater danger in a spiritual course when one runs along in it without the check of counsel and direction. In the *Conference of Abbot Moses*, Cassian observes: "By no other vice does the devil so lead a monk on in order to hurl him headlong to destruction, as when he persuades him to disregard the counsel of his superiors and trust to his own judgment and decision." (*Collationes*, II, c. 11. PL 49, col. 541.)

12   What is more, without this obedience of the intellect, obedience of the will and execution cannot possibly be what they should. For nature has so arranged matters that what are

called the appetitive powers of the soul must follow the apprehensive; and the will cannot long obey without violence when there is disagreement in the judgment. One may obey for some time perhaps, under the common misunderstanding that obey we must even if commanded amiss. But such obedience cannot last, with the resulting failure in perseverance, or at least in the perfection of obedience—which consists in obeying cheerfully and lovingly. And there can be no love or cheerfulness as long as such a conflict exists between action and judgment. We fail in zest and punctuality, when we question whether it is good or not to obey a command. We fail in that glorious simplicity of blind obedience, when we examine a command to see whether it is right or not, and even pass sentence against the superior because he asks us to do something we do not like. We fail in humility, because if from one point of view we obey, from another we prefer ourselves to our superior. We fail in courage in difficult tasks. In a word, all the perfection and dignity of this virtue is lost.

On the other hand, we have instead pain, discontent, delays, weariness, complaints, excuses and other faults which are far from trivial and completely strip obedience of its value and merit. It is this that leads St. Bernard to say, speaking of those who become disgruntled when the commands of the superior are little to their taste: "If you begin to grieve at this, to judge your superior, to murmur in your heart, even though you outwardly fulfil what is commanded, this is not the virtue of patience [= obedience], but a cloak over your malice." (*Sermo III, de Circumcisione,* n. 8. PL 183, col. 140.) Peace and tranquillity of soul he certainly shall not enjoy who has in his own heart the cause of his disturbance and unrest, I mean the conflict between his own judgment and the obligations of obedience.

13   This is why the Apostle, wishing to safeguard the spirit of unity, which is the binding force of every society, is so much in earnest when he urges all to be of one mind and

one heart. (Rom. 15:15; 1 Cor. 1:10; 2 Cor. 13:11; Phil. 2:2.) He knows that if the faithful agree in will and judgment, they will be a mutual and unfailing help to each other. Now if there must be one and the same understanding between the members and the head, it is easy to see whether it is more reasonable for the head to agree with the members, or the members with the head. From all I have thus far said, you can see quite clearly the absolute necessity of this obedience of the understanding.

14   But how perfect is this obedience, and at the same time how pleasing to God, can be seen from this, that what is most excellent in man and beyond all price is consecrated to God. Secondly, because one who thus obeys becomes a living holocaust, most pleasing to His Divine Majesty, seeing that he keeps nothing at all for himself. And finally because of the difficulty which the obedient man experiences in overcoming himself for God's love, since he resists the inclination which is natural to all men: to think for themselves and to follow their own opinion. From these considerations it follows that, although obedience seems to be a perfection of the will, since it makes it prompt and ready at the beck of the superior, yet it has to do also with the understanding itself, as we have pointed out, and should bring it to think what the superior thinks. Thus the whole power of the soul, its will and intelligence, will be brought to bear on a prompt and perfect performance of what is commanded.

15   I think I hear you say, beloved brethren, that you have no doubt about your needing this virtue, and that you would like very much to know how you can acquire it in its perfection. With St. Leo I answer, "To the humble nothing is hard, nothing difficult to the meek." (*Sermo 35*, c. 3. PL 54, col. 252.) If you have humility, if you have meekness, God will have the goodness to help you stand by your promise not only cheerfully but even lovingly.

16   In addition to these practices I especially recommend three others which will be a great help to you in your efforts to acquire this obedience of the understanding.

The first is that, as I said in the beginning, you do not take a personal view of your superior and think of him as a mere man, subject to error and adversity, but as Christ Himself Who is Supreme Wisdom, Boundless Goodness and Infinite Charity, Who can neither be deceived nor will deceive you. And since you are well aware that it was out of love for God that you have taken this yoke of obedience upon yourselves, in the thought that in carrying out the superior's will you would be more certain to be carrying out God's will, you should not have the slightest doubt that the most faithful love of God will continue to guide you by the hands of those whom He has placed over you. You should, therefore, listen to their words when they command you, as though they were the very words of Christ Himself. The Apostle, writing to the Colossians and encouraging subjects to be obedient to their superiors, says on this point: "Whatever you do, work at it from the heart as for the Lord and not for men, knowing that from the Lord you will receive the inheritance as your reward. Serve the Lord Christ." (Col. 3:23, 24.) And St. Bernard: "Whether it be God or man, His vicar, who commands anything, we must obey with equal diligence and show equal reverence, on the supposition, however, that man commands nothing that is contrary to God." (*Liber de praecepto et dispensatione*, c. 19. PL 182, col. 871.) Thus if you behold not man with the eyes of the body, but God with the eyes of the soul, you will surely not find it difficult to conform your will and judgment to that norm of conduct which you yourselves have chosen.

17   The second practice is that in your own mind you always make a serious effort to defend the superior's command, or even his thought, but never to find fault with it. To do this it will be a help if you are always favorably dis-

posed to any order he may give. You will thus obey, not only
without annoyance, but even with a glad heart, because, as
St. Leo tells us, "It is not hard to serve when we love what is
commanded." (*Sermo de jejunio septimi mensis*, iv. PL 54,
col. 444.)

18   There is a third and last way of bringing the judgment into subjection. It is easier and safer and much used by
the holy Fathers. Make up your minds that whatever the
superior commands is the command and will of God Himself.
Just as in accepting a truth which the Catholic Church puts
before you, you at once bring into play all the powers of
mind and heart, so in carrying out any order whatever of the
superior, you should be swept on by a kind of blind passion
to obey, without making even the slightest enquiry into the
command.[18] It is thus we must believe that Abraham acted
when he was told to offer his son, Isaac, in sacrifice. (Gen.
22:1-13.) Thus, in the days of the New Testament, some of
those holy fathers of whom Cassian speaks, as the abbot John
who without a single thought as to whether it would do any
good or not, with great and prolonged labor watered a dry
stick for a whole year on end, when told to do so: or whether
it was possible, when he strove so mightily to move a huge
rock which many men with their combined strength could
not have budged. (*De Institutis Renuntiantium*, lib. iv, cc. 25,
26. PL 49, col. 183.) We see that heaven sometimes approved
this kind of obedience with miracles. Not to mention others,
with whom you are well acquainted, Maurus the disciple of
St. Benedict, went into a lake on the order of his superior and
did not sink. (Sancti Gregorii M., *Lib. 2 Dialogorum, Vita
Sancti Benedicti*, c. 7. PL 66, col. 146.) Another, at the word
of his superior captured a lioness and brought her home. (*De
Vitis Patrum*, lib. iii, n. 27. PL 73, col. 755.) Now this manner
of subjecting one's judgment so as unhesitatingly to approve
or praise in one's own mind any command of the superior is
not only the practice of holy men, but must be imitated by

those who desire to practice perfect obedience in everything, except where sin is clearly involved.

19 But for all that, you are not forbidden to lay before your superior something that occurs to you and that seems to be at variance with his mind, and which you think might be called to his attention. You should, however, first consult the Lord in prayer. There is, of course, some danger of being deceived by self-love in such instances, and to guard against it and your own judgment you should, both before and after submitting your difficulty, be completely indifferent, not only with regard to undertaking or dropping the proposal itself, but you should be ready even to approve and think best whatever decision the Superior makes.

20 What I have said of obedience should be the practice of individuals towards their immediate superiors, and of rectors and local superiors towards their provincials, and of provincials towards the general, and of the general, finally, towards him whom God has placed over him, I mean, His vicar on earth. In this way a perfect subordination of authority will be maintained, with the resulting harmony and love, without which neither the proper government of our Society nor of any other congregation whatever could be preserved.

It is in this way that Divine Providence "ordereth all things sweetly" (Wisd. 8:1), leading to their particular ends the lowest by means of the midmost, and the midmost by means of the highest. Among the angels there is likewise this graded subordination of one hierarchy to another, and in the heavenly bodies and all their movements an orderly and close connection and interrelation is kept, all movement coming from the one Supreme Mover in perfect order, step by step, to the lowest.

We see the same thing on earth, not only in every civilized government, but especially in the Church's hierarchy, where officials and their activities draw their authority from the one universal Vicar of Christ our Lord. The better this subordination and gradation is kept, the better and smoother will be the government. But when it is absent, anyone can see how deplorable are the results wherever men are assembled together. It is my earnest desire, therefore, to see this virtue flourish as vigorously in this Society which God has to some extent entrusted to me, as though the well-being and continued existence of our Society depended on it alone.

21   Not to go beyond the limits I set myself at the beginning of this letter, I beg of you in the name of our Lord Jesus Christ, Who gave Himself to us not only as a teacher of obedience, but also as a model of it, to bend every effort to acquire this virtue, and, all athirst for so glorious a victory, to gain complete mastery over yourselves, that is, over the sublimest and most difficult part of your souls, your will, I mean, and understanding. For it is in this way that the true and solid knowledge of God our Lord will draw your souls to Him completely, and rule and govern you throughout the whole course of this mortal pilgrimage, until at last He leads you and many others who have been helped by your efforts and example to that last and most blissful end, which is life everlasting.

I earnestly commend myself to your prayers.

Rome, March 26, 1553.

To the Abbot of Salas
Francisco Jiménez de Miranda

Francisco Jiménez de Miranda, Abbot of Salas in the Province of Burgos, was living in sacrilegious union in Rome from 1554 to 1556, and was also making illicit use of ecclesiastical revenues he held. He wished to found a college in Burgos and entrust it to the Society in atonement for his sins. But he kept putting off the carrying out of his purpose because of the difficulties his own sins put in his way and the covetousness of a brother, who claimed the Abbot's income for himself and for his children. St. Ignatius, with the disinterestedness which will appear, had the conversion of this unfortunate man much at heart. To obtain this grace the fathers in Rome said two Masses daily. Besides having recourse to God, the saint endeavored by means of visits, letters, and so on, to have this old man make a radical change in his life, and he succeeded to the extent of removing the occasion of his sins from his house. The unhappy man, nevertheless, clung to his evil ways, and refused to receive the visits or answer the letters of the saint. Ignatius finally sent him the following letter, a witness of his unselfish, courageous and untiring apostolic zeal.

Rome, July 11, 1555

IHS

My very Reverend and Honorable Lord in Jesus Christ:

As I have not been able to gain admittance to your presence, either by messenger, note or personal call, I might easily give up from weariness if I were looking for something for myself. But as I am sincerely seeking something that has to do with God's service and your salvation, I should not yield to weariness, or give up trying to accomplish by letter what I could not do by word of mouth, if the least vestige of charity remained in me.

My Lord, what urges me most is not to get the college in Burgos started. God will bring that about in His own time by someone or other, since it is a work of such great service to God. I do indeed desire that Your Worship be the founder, and, seeing that we have done everything possible to satisfy your conditions, even to our Father's offering to turn over to Your Lordship's disposal the houses we now possess there, I have nothing further to ask in this matter. What hurts me most is the continual pains you resort to in what concerns the welfare of your soul, as I see that in this negligence there is a very great and imminent danger. As I love you in Christ our Lord, and daily beg God for your salvation in my Masses and prayers, I cannot help feeling a great sorrow until I behold you once more travelling on the road to salvation. I am aware of your advanced years, I am aware of the condition of your health, your disposition, your physical ailments, which are such that when we least expect it, death may overtake you. What would cause me extreme anguish is that death should find you unprovided with the penance which your sins demand, and with the good and pious works that are necessary, if you are to attain to eternal happiness.

My Lord, this is no time for pretenses with those who love you. Do not look upon him as a friend or servant, but as a mortal enemy of your soul, who attends you with flattery, especially those who reassure you and hold you in your sins. What you need is penance and much of it.

This means that you must not only withdraw from your sin and be sorry for it, but that you must make satisfaction for past sins, and unburden your conscience of so much

Church property that has been misappropriated. I am not talking about injustice *in foro externo,* but of Church property which is not necessary for the support of your state, and which belongs to the poor and to pious works. According to the holy doctors it is a great injustice to deprive them of these goods. It will not be enough that the Rota or the papal tribunals give you the possession and the enjoyment of these revenues when you come to stand before the tribunal of Christ our Lord, Who will have to demand of you a strict accounting of all that you have taken from the Church. Very soon it will be necessary for you to appear in person before His Infinite Justice to await a peremptory sentence from which there will be no appeal. It will be either to a happy and most blessed life, full of joy and consolation and inestimable honor, or to a most unhappy death and eternal damnation, full of all the miseries and torments which the rigor and severity of Divine Justice have prepared for those who die impenitent and without having made satisfaction for their sins.

You do not know whether you will be summoned to this judgment this coming September, or this month, or this very night. Many a man in better health than you enjoy, more conservative in his personal habits, has gone to bed without a care, and was not alive when morning came. Do not put your soul in such peril. By the love of Jesus Christ, by the Blood He shed to redeem your soul, make ready to give a good account of yourself and of all that God our Lord has given you to dispense. As He has awaited you this long with so much mercy, do not allow the short time of life that remains to slip by fruitlessly, so that you find yourself at the last moment, when you would give everything you have and all that the world is worth for an hour in which to repent and do good. And it will not be given you, if now in the time granted you by the wisdom of God, you refuse to help yourself.

You will pardon my straightforward speech. But my love

constrains me, and I should not want my conscience to accuse me of having omitted this service expected of one who is devoted to you and who desires your eternal salvation. Every day, most unworthy though I am, I beg God's supreme clemency, and I feel that you lack those who should remind you of your duty. I know that there are some who speak otherwise, let alone the fact that the flesh and the devil add their contribution.

I am so anxious to see you dispose yourself for the grace of God our Lord by good and pious works, that if you thought our college ought to be deferred in favor of any other work you had in mind for the relief of your conscience and your own greater merit in the eyes of our Lord, I would readily agree. But it would not be a good work to bestow wealth on one's relatives who already have enough according to their state; nor to set up monuments of little spiritual advantage and little help for the common good. To give to the poor and to pious works is what raises everlasting monuments in heaven for the enjoyment of those who make them, while for those which are worldly and vain, they merit torment and the severest pain. You should remember that you are not absolute master of your possessions, but their steward, and that you will be held accountable for them. This will suffice for one of your understanding.

Here we do not, and will not cease to ask God's goodness in behalf of Your Lordship, whether you thank us or not. God is our end, and these many years now I have been a kind of chaplain of yours, although you do not look upon me as such, or give me credit for my good intention. It is enough, however, to have God and my conscience for witness. May the Holy Spirit be with Your Lordship.

From this your own house, July 11, 1555.

Notes

Notes

The substance of these notes has been taken from the *Monumenta Ignatiana* (MHSI), Ser. 4, *Fontes Narrativi*, Vol. 1.

AUTHOR'S PREFACE

1. His reluctance to speak of his Jerusalem pilgrimage was due to the distinction attached at the time to such pilgrims. He was anxious to avoid every occasion of self-complacence.

2. This refers to the plans for a mission to Ethiopia, the emperor of which the Portuguese and others at the time thought was the famous Prester John.

3. Marcellus II (Cervini) was elected pope April 9, 1555 and died the 30th of the same month.

4. Paul IV (Pietro Carafa), elected May 23, 1555.

5. A small dwelling adjoining the professed house at Rome, frequently used as an infirmary.

CHAPTER 1

1. The castle of Pamplona.

2. Who this lady was is not clearly known. From the wording of the Spanish text her station was higher than that of countess or duchess. Some have suggested Queen Germaine, widow of Ferdinand; others, the Princess Catherine, sister of Charles V.

3. A monastery of the Carthusians was near Burgos and is still standing.

4. The date of his departure from home is not certain.

CHAPTER 2

1. This was probably his priest brother, Pero López de Loyola, who lived until 1527.

2. A shrine dedicated to our Lady near Oñate. It was later destroyed by fire. In a letter to St. Francis Borgia, August 20, 1554, St. Ignatius speaks of it with affection and refers to this vigil as having been the occasion of some spiritual advantage to him.

3. The name of this sister is not known for certain. It was probably Magdalena who had married Juan López de Gallaiztegui.

4. This was Father Juan de Chanones (Chanon), a Frenchman.

CHAPTER 3

1. This is the first appearance in the life of St. Ignatius of the practice of frequent communion, a practice he promoted throughout all the rest of his life. It may have been recommended to him by Dom Chanones who according to his obituary notice was wont to celebrate Mass daily.

2. In Books of Hours three prayers were frequently given, one to each of the Divine Persons, and then a fourth to the Most Holy Trinity.

3. Father Nonell, in *Manresa Ignaciana*, page 76, note 1, thinks that this man is the son of Anthony Benedict and Joanna Ferrer. A fuller discussion of the point can be found in *Fontes Narrativi*, p. 408, note 29.

4. Baltasar de Faria was a business representative in Rome of the King of Portugal from 1543 to 1551.

5. These pious and noble ladies who took a special interest in Ignatius at Manresa were Agnes Pascual, Angela Amigant, Michaela Canyelles, Agnes Clavera, and Brianda Paguera. Their names appear in the process for canonization held at Manresa in 1595.

6. One of the noblest families of Catalonia.

7. The smallest Spanish coin current at the time.

CHAPTER 4

1. The fact that she understood Ignatius speaking Spanish suggests that the lady was Joanna of Aragon, the wife of Asconio

Colonna, and the city in which Ignatius found hospitality, Paliano. But there is no reason for thinking that he could not be understood by an Italian woman even if he spoke Spanish. Father Tacchi Venturi thinks that the city was Fondi and the lady, Beatrice Appiani, wife of Vespasiano Colonna.

2. From the accounts of others who made the pilgrimage this year, 1553, we learn that the Doge was Andrea Gritti.

3. The pilgrims apparently reached Jaffa August 24-25, but were forbidden to land until the 31st. They entered Jerusalem September 4th, and apparently remained until September 23rd.

4. Father Angelo de Ferrara. Properly speaking he was the Guardian of the monastery of Mount Sion. These were the superiors of all the monasteries in Palestine and were also called Provincials.

CHAPTER 5

1. September 23, 1523. Because of difficulties raised by the Turks they did not reach Jaffa until October 3rd, and setting out from there, cast anchor in the port of Salinas, Cyprus, on the 14th.

2. The master of the vessel was Jerome Contarini.

3. About one-fourth of a ducat.

4. War was being waged between Francis I and Charles V and his allies over the possession of the Duchy of Milan. In the beginning of 1524, however, military activities were almost at a standstill.

5. Andrea Dória (1466-1560), the famous Genoese seaman. In 1522 he was fighting on the side of the French King, but after the battle of Pavia in 1525, he espoused the cause of Clement VII. Finally, in 1528, he joined Charles V and remained a friend of the Spaniards until death.

CHAPTER 6

1. This man was a monk of the order of St. Bernard, that is, a Cistercian. Other than that we know nothing about him.

2. The new University of Alcalá de Henares had been founded a few years earlier, in 1508, by Francisco Ximénez de Cisneros, Archbishop of Toledo, and had attracted a large student body.

3. At Barcelona, Ignatius had already gathered as companions Callistus Sa, Lope de Cáceres, and Arteaga.

4. The "Illuminati" were generally understood to be those who, putting too much trust in the light they fancied they had received from heaven, either made little of ecclesiastical authority, or, paying little heed to the moral law, allowed themselves to be involved in crime and vice, especially the vice of the flesh.

5. In the judgment, Ignatius and his companions were not ordered to dye their clothing differently, but to change it. When Ignatius says here and later that he and his companions were ordered to dye their garments, we should suppose that the vicar, moved by the request of Ignatius and his companions or some of their friends, softened the judgment.

6. Teresa Enriquez (1456?-1529), wife of Gutierres de Cárdenas, was well known for her generosity to the poor and to captives, and for her devotion to the Blessed Sacrament.

7. Dr. Pedro Ciruelo, an Aragonese from Daroca, philosopher, theologian and mathematician of great authority in the University of Alcalá. He had been appointed by the founder himself, Fray Ximénes de Cisneros, the first lecturer in the chair of St. Thomas. A few years later he went to Salamanca, where he is said to have died.

8. There was a college founded by Fonseca at Salamanca for poor scholars, called St. James' or the Archbishop's.

CHAPTER 7

1. St. Ignatius had not actually devoted a full year and a half to higher studies, as he was prevented from doing so by his spiritual activities and his imprisonment. We should note, however, that the spiritual activities, visits especially, were carried out on feast days, not on ordinary week days, which he devoted to study.

2. Desiderius Erasmus of Rotterdam, the best known humanist writer of his age, had many supporters and many adversaries in Spain at the time.

3. Counting the days Ignatius was at Salamanca before his imprisonment, which lasted twenty-two days, and the days he remained after his liberation, he could hardly have been there two

months, perhaps from mid-July to mid-September. He probably did not matriculate at the University, where classes began October 18th.

CHAPTER 8

1. Writing from Paris to Agnes Pascual, March 3, 1528, Ignatius says: "I arrived here at Paris February 2nd in good time and sound health, thanks to the grace and goodness of God our Lord."

2. The College of Montagu was situated on the left bank of the Seine, where the Bibliothèque Sainte-Geneviève now stands, not far from the Panthéon.

3. The Hospital of St. James was founded at the beginning of the fourteenth century for pilgrims on the way to Compostella, Spain. It was situated on the right bank of the river on the site now occupied by a private dwelling at 133 rue St. Denis, near the rue du Cygne, and not far from the Church of St. Leu-St. Gilles. It might be worth noting that lectures began at Montagu at four in the morning, with the last lecture at half-past seven in the evening.

4. Diego de Gouvea was dean of the College of Sainte-Barbe. St. Ignatius is silent about the outcome of the threats of Master Gouvea. Ribadeneira tells us that Gouvea later changed his purpose of punishing Ignatius into praise of him.

5. Leonora Mascarenhas (Mascareñas) (1503-1581), a young noblewoman of Portugal, had come to Spain in the train of the Empress Elizabeth, wife of Charles V. She was the governess of Prince Philip. Until her death she was always a supporter of St. Ignatius and the Society.

6. As to the studies that Ignatius made at Paris, we must remember that he studied grammar and humanities from February 1528 to September 1529; arts or philosophy, 1529-1530, 1530-1531, 1531-1532. From October 1532 to Easter 1533, according to the custom of the University of Paris, he must have undergone a number of tests preliminary to receiving the Master's degree. In the year 1533, after receiving his degree, he could devote himself to theology, and all of the year 1534 and 1535 up to the month of April, when he returned to Spain. In 1536 the theological faculty testified that Ignatius had studied theology for a year and a half.

CHAPTER 9

1. Martin García de Oñaz y Loyola, after the death of the eldest brother, Juan Pérez de Loyola (who made his will at Naples, June 21, 1496, and died there), became lord of the house of Loyola. He married Magdalena de Araoz, September 14, 1493, and died November 29, 1538.

2. The hospital was called the *Magdalena* and was situated on the outskirts of Azpeitia.

3. One of these was his nephew Beltran de Loyola, to whom he gave the Spiritual Exercises, as may be gathered from a letter addressed to him in February of 1542.

4. Khaïr-Ed-Dîn, a well known pirate in the Mediterranean, was at the head of Soliman II's fleet.

CHAPTER 10

1. Pietro Contarini was a noble Venetian cleric, treasurer of the Hospital of the Incurables. In 1543, John Matthew Giberti, Bishop of Verona, on his deathbed, recommended him as his successor. The Venetian Senate made every effort, but without success, to have this nomination confirmed by the Supreme Pontiff. In 1557 Contarini was named Bishop of Paphos, on the island of Cyprus, a see which he resigned in 1562, while he was at the Council of Trent, in favor of Francesco Contarini. Pietro, whether he was nephew or not of Cardinal Gaspar Contarini, was of great help to the infant Society with the Cardinal.

2. In Decoudray's Latin version he is called *Cettinus*, which in the processes of Madrid and Alcalá is found in the Latin form *Septensi*. There is really question here of the city of Mauritania which today is known as Ceuta.

3. Dr. Ortiz and John Peter Carafa. See above ¶93.

4. This is confirmed by what St. Ignatius wrote in his *Journal* for February 23, 1544. ". . . it seems to me that this appearance and perception of Jesus had something to do with the Most Holy Trinity, as it came to mind when the Father placed me with His Son."

5. A fuller account has come to us from Laynez. It was given by him in a community exhortation at Rome in the year 1559.

This was published by Tacchi Venturi, *Storia* I, 586. The account of this vision differs in details as given by Laynez, Nadal, and others. The apparition took place at *La Storta*, a village on the Via Cassia, about fourteen kilometers from the Porta Populi, on the road from Siena to Rome. The chapel was repaired in 1700 by Thyrso González, General of the Society, and a memorial plaque placed over the entrance.

CHAPTER II

1. In the beginning of 1538. Because of a lack of contemporary documents the time cannot be more precisely estimated. According to a tradition existing at Monte Cassino, Ignatius gave the spiritual exercises to Dr. Ortiz, not in the great monastery, but in a nearby priory, which depended on the monastery and was called *Santa Maria dell'Albaneta*.

2. Hocez was the first of Ignatius' companions to die. Codure tells us that in life he was very dark and anything but handsome, but after death became as beautiful as an angel. See also ¶92.

3. This was the property of Quirino Garzoni and was close to the *Trinitá dei Monti*.

4. Among those who made the Spiritual Exercises under St. Ignatius, Polanco numbers Dr. Pedro Ortiz, Lactantio Tolomei, Dr. Iñigo López and Cardinal Gaspar Contarini. From Quirino's vineyard to St. Mary Major, and thence to the Ponte Sesto and back to the vineyard is a walk of about two hours or a little less. Thus if he gave the points of meditation once, and visited them once later, he spent almost four hours going and coming.

5. He is usually called Michael Navarro, but seems to be the same person as Michael Landivar.

6. Benedict Conversini from Pistoia was elected Bishop of Bartinoro in central Italy. In 1540 he was transferred to the see of Jesi, and made Governor of the City, March 21, 1538. He died in 1553.

7. As late as April 6, 1555, Ignatius wrote to recommend him to Father Pelletier, then living at Ferrara. On January 7, 1556, he tried to get a letter from Juan de Vega, Viceroy of Sicily, to the Supreme Pontiff in favor of Mudarra.

8. Barrera is little known. Ribadeneira says that he disavowed his error and died shortly after the persecution ended. He seems to have been still living at the end of 1539.

9. Vincent Carafa, Cardinal of Naples. He was raised to the purple by Clement VII November 21, 1527, was appointed legate of the City by Paul III March 20, 1538, and died August 28, 1541. As legate of the City he gave faculties to the first fathers, May 3, 1538, to preach and exercise other sacred functions.

10. All that has come down to us from the *Diary* or *Journal* of St. Ignatius (how much has been lost we do not know) has been published lately in the *Monumenta Ignatiana, Constitutiones* I, 86-158. It begins February 2, 1544 and ends February 27, 1545. It includes therefore almost thirteen months. Up to the 4th of April, that is, for about two months the notes are fairly long, and in them Ignatius speaks of the heavenly visions he had and of the mystical consolations he experienced. From April 5th on to the end (except for May 11, 12, 13 and 22) the notes are very brief and contain nothing, openly at least, about visions or revelations. There is scarcely anything else but indications of tears or interior mystical discourse.

Notes to the Letters

1. A lady of Barcelona with something of a shrewish disposition. Her name was Leonor Zapila Rocaberti. Ignatius' first meeting with her is recounted in Dudon, *Life of St. Ignatius Loyola* (Milwaukee; Bruce, 1949), p. 72.

2. Ignatius here alludes to a jurisdictional dispute instituted by the Franciscans and settled by a bull of Leo X, which handed over the visitation of the monastery of Santa Clara to the Benedictines.

3. Gennadius, *De ecclesiasticis dogmatibus*, a book which was attributed to St. Augustine.

4. The author of the book *De Sacramentis* (lib. 5, c. 4), attributed to St. Ambrose, whose teaching on this subject is given in a sermon which was numbered among St. Augustine's: "Receive daily what daily benefits you. So live as to merit to receive daily. He who does not merit to receive daily, does not merit to receive yearly."

5. Ps. 18:13, "From my secret sins cleanse me, O Lord."

6. 1 Cor. 4:4, "For I am not conscious to myself of anything. Yet I am not thereby justified: but he that judgeth me is the Lord."

7. John 14:6, "I am the Way . . ."

8. Object, that is, God, Who is offended.

9. November 16, 1545 five young Jesuits had come from Portugal to Gandia.

10. Leonor de Castro, wife of Francis Borgia.

11. Juana de Meneses. This placing the Society in the possession of its friends is an expression of courtesy common in Spain. A host will assure his guest that the house is his. St. Ignatius makes frequent use of such expressions.

12. Ignatius is apparently referring to Antonio de Muñiz. His name recurs in the Letters. Unfortunately, he left the Society later.

It was some eight or ten months later that Francis Borgia himself asked to be received into the Society.

13. The name appears in a variety of forms: Doimus, sometimes Doymus, with greater freedom in the surname, Nascius, Naucius, Nascio and Naggio. He was a warm friend of the Society. In 1556 he presented the Society with a house in Ameria, and even wished to make a gift of himself. After he had been a few days in probation in 1555, it was thought better for him to serve God without the obligation of obedience. This was not the first time that Ignatius was consigned to the flames. One wonders whether his thought did not go back to the days of Alcalá, when a similar incident happened, pithily related by Pere Dudon. (*Life of St. Ignatius Loyola,* English translation [Milwaukee; Bruce], p. 117.)

14. Perpignan at the extreme north-east corner of Spain, and Seville at the south-west, would seem to indicate every Jesuit in Spain.

15. Ignatius here recalls the teaching of St. Thomas, III, q. 87, a. 3.

16. PL here and hereafter in the text refers to Migne's *Patrologia Latina.*

17. The term "spiritual father" here means superior. Later it was reserved to designate the spiritual director, an office now quite distinct from that of superior.

18. The misunderstanding concerning "blind" obedience is rather widespread. But the practice is common even today and on the natural level, as anyone with any experience of doctors or hospitals can testify. On the supernatural level it is practiced in and out of religion when the commands of legitimate authority are obeyed without questioning their prudence, timeliness, etc., it being always supposed that nothing evidently evil or wrong is involved. When the subject's only reason for obeying is that he is commanded and he obeys without a thought of the agreeableness of the command, simply making the superior's will and judgment his own, he obeys blindly. The examples given in the text are certainly extreme, and no superior would be justified in lightly making similar demands on his or her subjects.